the king retired to his apartments in the Palace of Whitehall and the arms of his mistress, Barbara Villiers, Mrs Palmer. She was the latest and one of the most long-lasting of the king's conquests; there was a steadily increasing clutch of royal bastards, of which James Crofts was the eldest and most favoured. Barbara, like Lucy Walter before her, had made her way to the court-in-exile

Barbara Palmer, née Villiers (later Countess of Castlemaine) as a shepherdess, after Sir Peter Lely. (*Yale Center for British Art, Paul Mellon Collection*)

via a series of lovers and there she snared a rich husband, Roger Palmer, before being noticed by the king. She ruled Charles II's heart and later the Palace of Whitehall as a *maîtresse-en-titre* (mistress to the king) in the fashion of Louis XIV's French court where it was a semi-official position.

Prince Rupert of the Rhine, studio of Sir Peter Lely. (*Yale Center for British Art, Paul Mellon Collection*)

The new reign was soon beset by tragedy. Disease spread like wildfire in the crowded capital and in August 1660, during a smallpox epidemic that reached the royal court, the king's younger brother Henry, Duke of Gloucester died aged 20. A month later Charles's sister Mary, Princess of Orange, arrived in London. On Christmas Eve, she too lost her life to the same disease as her younger brother. The princess's dying wish - a futile one – was that Charles be guardian to her young son. While this wasn't to be, the king did interest himself in his nephew's welfare and career, as did the boy's godfather, Prince Rupert, now returned to England and one of Charles II's most trusted inner circle.

Dropping like a bombshell into the turmoil of the royal family's private life, it was discovered that the king's remaining brother, James, Duke of York, had made a secret and illicit marriage. With no legitimate offspring (Lucy's claims for her son aside), the duke was Charles's heir and so was expected to make a good marriage. Before the restoration, the duke's lover – to whom he had proposed on a romantic whim – had fallen pregnant. This was no woman easily swept under the carpet as Lucy Walter had been, or one prepared to live in the public eye as a mistress in the vein of Barbara, Mrs Palmer. She was the 23-year-old daughter of the king's chief advisor, Edward Hyde. Just over three months after Charles had entered London in triumph, James, Duke of York and Anne Hyde were married with subterfuge and in the middle of the night. While the king knew (he had, after some persuasion, given his permission), very few other people did. This included Henrietta Maria, who was enraged when she was told that her new daughter-in-law was a commoner by birth. Despite this difficult start, in time Anne impressed everyone including her difficult mother-in-law, and James adored her, although it didn't stop his philandering ways. The diarist Samuel Pepys would later remark with splendid acidity 'that the Duke of York, in all things but his codpiece, is led by the nose by his wife.' The duke was a paler version of his older brother: while the quicksilver Charles was tall, dark and handsome, clever and crafty, the duke was a lumpy, sallow man who insisted on boring anyone who would listen with an almost obsessive discourse on anything naval or military. What the siblings shared was a love of masculine pursuits: sports, yachting, hunting and womanizing. Minette too had married and in Henrietta Maria's eyes it was a good match, although the young bride grew to view it in a different light. Her husband was Louis XIV of France's younger brother, the handsome but flamboyantly bisexual, cross-dressing Philippe, duc d'Orléans. The glittering French king, who would become known as the Sun King, was then beginning his ambitious project to transform a small hunting lodge at Versailles into a grand palace. In the meantime, the duc and new duchesse d'Orléans had their own court at the Palais Royale and, in London, the Duke of York followed the French fashion and presided over a smaller-scale court of his own.

Outside the confines of the palace, Charles II dispensed with diplomacy and was exacting a bloody vengeance on the men responsible for his father's death. In the words of one of the regicides, the lawyer, Augustine Garland, Charles I's trial had taken place in a period 'when the Government was thus tossed, and turned, and tumbled, and I know not what', but Charles was determined to punish all fifty-nine men still living who had signed his father's death warrant as well as the men who had sat in judgement and the executioner. Some were sentenced to life imprisonment and one or two managed to escape abroad where they lived in hiding, but many met a traitor's death. Colonel Adrian Scrope, Mary, Lady St John's relation, believed himself safe from retribution. He surrendered under a promise that he would be exempt from further punishment, but this decision was overturned. Scrope, now a 'comely ancient gentleman', was tried and found guilty of treason; five days later he was hung, drawn and quartered at Charing Cross. On the twelfth anniversary of Charles I's death, Oliver Cromwell's body was exhumed and his remains hung in a gibbet at Tyburn before being beheaded. The severed head was stuck on a pike on Westminster Hall and his body flung into a common pit. Exactly a year later, and on the same day every year thereafter, Robert Wallop MP, owner of the manor of Basing after its fall in the Civil War, suffered his punishment for being declared a regicide. Although Wallop had not signed Charles I's death warrant, he had attended the trial and the new king's retribution was wide-reaching. Confessing his guilt, Wallop suffered the public humiliation of being drawn once a year through the streets of London on a sled to the Tyburn gallows with a halter around his neck before being returned to the Tower where he was imprisoned for life.[1]

The new king rewarded those who had remained loyal to him or who had served him well at the Restoration. As well as positions in his household, there were new peerages created. General Monck became the Duke of Albemarle, and Hyde was made Earl of Clarendon. Anthony Ashley Cooper, who had been guardian to the Powlett children, had supported Monck and was given the title of Baron Ashley of Wimborne St Giles. Later he would succeed Hyde as Chancellor of the Exchequer and in 1672 was created the 1st Earl of Shaftesbury. There was a notable absence in the list of the men favoured by the king. Despite the Powlett family's sacrifices in support of the Royalist cause, they received scant reward in the early days of the new reign. If Lord St John was hoping for titles or a position at court, then he was disappointed. The elderly Marquess of Winchester cared little for a dukedom; he was more concerned with regaining his former estates and being compensated for his losses than taking centre stage in the world of politics or the new court and although his estates were returned to him – it was ordered that all confiscated lands be returned to their original owners, kick-starting a flurry of lawsuits and private Parliamentary bills – the marquess never did get any financial benefit. Although he was awarded 10,000*l.* in damages, the money failed to materialize and the marquess remained at Englefield House. When returned to the family, Basing House was uninhabitable. Despite the king's insistence on religious tolerance, the old marquess, defiantly and staunchly Catholic throughout the Interregnum, felt himself sidelined. He had lost almost everything during the Civil War and now faced a fight in his dotage if he wanted to reclaim what was due to him. Lord St John was returned as MP for Winchester in the year of the Restoration and for Hampshire the following year, but studiously avoided court life. It was an exuberant and hard-drinking clique of young men, bucks, libertines, chancers and rakehells who laid claim to the 'Merry Monarch's' presence, most of them up to their eyeballs in debt. Gambling, dancing and womanizing became part of daily life and Charles II's licentious court quickly became a byword for immorality. Pepys, who was no ardent royalist, claimed 'the King do nothing but pleasure, and hates the very sight or thoughts of business'. Given the sacrifice made by the Powlett family in Charles I's cause, the marquess and his eldest son received little in the way of any reward at the Restoration, a fact that sowed seeds of discontent.

For the new king, the most pressing matters of concern were his coronation and the hunt across Europe for a suitable bride. The first proved easier. Charles was crowned in Westminster Abbey on 23 April 1661 (the date symbolic as it was also the feast day of England's patron saint, St George) in an outpouring of celebratory jubilation. The royal regalia of his father's coronation had been broken up during the Interregnum, the gemstones sold off and the rest reduced to puddles of molten gold and silver before being turned into coins, but replicas had been made. In an age when portents and omens were taken seriously, the sun shone on the new king, at least for most of the day. Torrential rain and thunderstorms in the evening prevented the planned fireworks. Opinion remained divided as to whether God was expressing his joy or displeasure at the day's events.

The quest for a queen was problematic. Charles refused to consider any woman who had turned him down while he was exiled (they had been given their chance and missed it), and shied away from the Protestant German princesses suggested by his council. The last thing his advisors wanted was a Catholic bride, but Charles favoured a closer alliance with France and Louis XIV. After all, he had spent most of his exiled youth in France, his mother's homeland and his sister Minette's adopted country, and felt an affinity with the Sun King's court. That plan stalled too and all hopes came to rest on the diminutive shoulders of a Catholic Portuguese princess.

Short in stature and pretty enough to look at, Catherine of Braganza's main attraction was the small fortune she brought with her as a dowry (although, to the exasperation of the British, a portion was paid in sugar and spices rather than much-needed cash). Catherine also brought with her new territories in the form of Tangier and Bombay to add to the British dominions. Mrs Palmer caused a fuss and was placated with a title of the Irish peerage, giving her a countess's coronet when the long-suffering Robert Palmer was made Earl of Castlemaine against his wishes (he knew the title was really granted to Barbara, the wording making it clear it could descend only to her children and not those of any future marriage he might make). Making the most of being Lady Castlemaine, Barbara inveigled herself into position as one of the new queen's ladies and retained her rooms at Whitehall where Charles continued to visit her and their children. Barbara gave birth to her second child by Charles, a son, just weeks after his marriage to Catherine. Four more children were to follow (the last was probably John Churchill, later Duke of Marlborough's offspring, despite Barbara's claims to the contrary). Catherine of Braganza might have been small, but she was feisty and determined not to let Barbara usurp her position. Once she had mastered the English language, the new queen pleased the court with her modesty, the yin to Lady Castlemaine's yang, and Charles was fond of her. The king's eldest son arrived hot on the heels of the new queen. James Crofts, 'the King's bastard, a most pretty spark of about 15 years old' as Pepys described him (although he was 13), arrived at court, charming everyone he met and his father most of all. James danced with Lady Castlemaine and played cards with the queen and her ladies and was everyone's favourite. In no time, Charles created his son Duke of Monmouth (the title Earl of Monmouth had lapsed in 1661 with the death of Henry Carey, the 2nd Earl and the father of Lady St John's first husband, Lord Leppington). A marriage was arranged to a wealthy 12-year-old Scottish heiress, Anne Scott, Countess of Buccleuch in her own right. Under the terms of Anne's father's

Catherine of Braganza, print after Jan Baptist Gaspars. (*Yale Center for British Art, Paul Mellon Collection*)

will, her husband had to take her surname and James happily obliged; he was thereafter James Scott. As a wedding gift, and in opposition to his advisors, the king made his son and new wife the Duke and Duchess of Buccleuch, but James continued to be known as Monmouth. The two children maintained separate households until they were old enough to live together as man and wife; James remained at Whitehall by his father's side, learning to ape the king in all things, including his womanizing ways. Charles II's attention had wandered from Lady Castlemaine when a new arrival at court eclipsed even Barbara's beauty and caught his eye. Frances Stuart, *la belle Stuart*, was just a few months older than his son but, despite her youth, she managed to keep the amorous king at arm's length.[2]

Lord and Lady St John's family had grown and a second daughter, Mary and a son, Charles had joined Jane in the Powletts' nursery. A larger house had become a necessity, and one in London would place St John closer to the royal court. The Honourable Charles Rich (later the 4th Earl of Warwick) owned a commodious house on Arch Row, the western side of Lincoln's Inn Fields in the parish of St Giles-in-the-Fields. A staunch Parliamentarian, his uncle Robert Rich had been – for a short time – married to Cromwell's youngest daughter Frances (Robert Rich died of consumption less than three months after their wedding) and his uncle, the 1st Earl of Holland, had been guardian of the Scrope children until he was imprisoned by Colonel Adrian Scrope (and subsequently executed). Now, after his only child (a son) had died of smallpox at the Arch Row house, Charles Rich was unable to bear living there. Within two months the house was sold. It was acquired by a man whose allegiances were a world away from those held by Charles Rich; the buyer was Lord St John and it was in this house that Francis Nicholson undertook the duties of a page to St John's wife.[3]

The square gardens of Lincoln's Inn Fields had been laid out and designed by Inigo Jones following a commission from James I. At the time Lord St John lived there, the east side was yet to be built; the west side was known as Arch Row, the north Newman's and the south Portugal Row. Later known as Lindsey House and now as Nos 59 and 60 Lincoln's Inn Fields, during St John's occupation his mansion was called Winchester House and was one of the grandest of the houses facing the square (it remained in the family until 1685 when it was sold). Almost certainly the house was the work of Inigo Jones who was responsible for several properties on the west and southern aspects of Lincoln's Inn Fields. Next door to St John was Edward Montagu, 1st Earl of Sandwich and formerly one of Cromwell's closest associates, but a

James Scott, Duke of Monmouth, engraving of the portrait by Sir Peter Lely. (*Yale University Art Gallery*)

man with the wit to see which way the wind blew. He had secretly contacted Charles II ahead of the Restoration and, as he was innocent of any part in Charles I's trial and execution, Montagu was rewarded with his earldom and various official positions, including an appointment as Lord High Admiral of

England, much to Prince Rupert's disgust. (Rupert refused to serve jointly with Montagu.) Samuel Pepys was a regular visitor to Montagu's house in Lincoln's Inn Fields, writing in his diary that it was 'a fine house, but deadly dear' as the rent was 250*l*. per annum. Across the green open space of the Fields (a notorious haunt for prostitutes and thieves) stood the Duke's Theatre in a building once used as a 'real tennis' court. During Cromwell's tenure at the helm, entertainments had been banned. Now a new atmosphere prevailed and, with the king's whole-hearted encouragement, the theatres reopened across the capital. The Duke's Theatre was, as its name suggests, under the patronage of the king's brother, the Duke of York and was managed by Sir William Davenant (named as William Shakespeare's godson, although popular rumour at the time hinted that he was Shakespeare's son). Largely ignored by the privileged inhabitants, the large parish of St Giles-in-the-Fields (in which Lord St John's new home was situated) had a seedy underbelly. To the west, a short distance from the newly-built luxury of Arch Row, many inhabitants lived in abject poverty.[4]

Every year there were a few cases of the plague, the disease carried and spread by bites from infected fleas in the fur of black rats, but there had not been

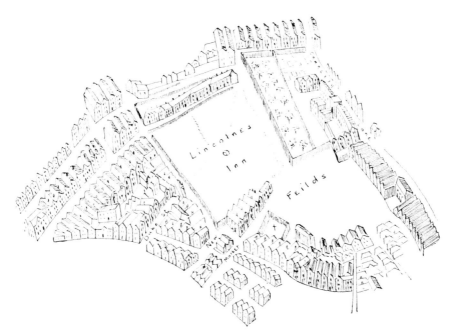

Map of Lincoln's Inn Fields, c.1658. (*British Library: Flickr*)

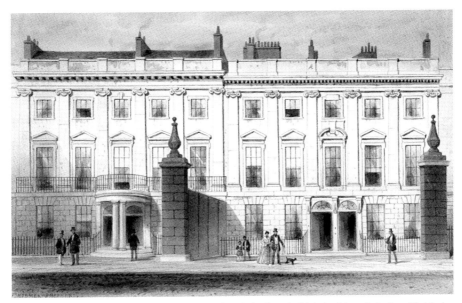

A later depiction of Lindsey House (on the right-hand side) in Lincoln's Inn Fields by Thomas Hosmer Shepherd. (*Authors' own collection*)

a major outbreak for almost three decades. The inhabitants of Lincoln's Inn Fields thought little of it when, towards the very end of 1664, there was a death attributed to plague in their parish. The unlucky victim lived at the northern end of Drury Lane, about a ten-minute walk from Winchester House and far enough removed not to cause concern. For a while, at least …

It appeared to be an isolated incident. No other cases were reported until February when there was another plague death in the parish, then another two in April, just after Charles II had visited the theatre at Lincoln's Inn Fields with Lady Castlemaine, little suspecting the disaster about to unfold. With a creeping slowness that lulled suspicion, other London parishes began to record fatalities. The death toll might still have stayed low but for the summer heatwave. The preceding winter had been cold and dry, followed by an equally dry spring, conditions that proved favourable to the plague-carrying black rats which bred and multiplied at an alarming rate. Now an epidemic of the plague broke out in London: by September, at its peak, all but four of London's 130 parishes remained free from the disease and more than 7,000 people were dying each week. St Giles-in-the-Fields was one of the worst hit parishes. The pest carts rumbled up and down the narrow lanes and streets during the long hot summer evenings, carrying stinking corpses to the mass grave pits for burial.

Lindsey House, now Nos 59-60 Lincoln's Inn Fields (right-hand side of image). (*Yale Center for British Art, Paul Mellon Collection*)

Infected houses bore a garish red cross painted on the door and the words 'Lord have mercy on us'. Anyone who was able to had closed up their houses and businesses and left for the countryside, but the disease spread like wildfire and followed in their wake, its tentacles spreading across the country. Noisy, bustling, vibrant London with its overcrowded medieval streets became a silent ghost city. The theatres closed their doors, traders shut up shop, street vendors ceased to call their wares in the streets and people stayed at home unless it was necessary to venture out. Pepys wrote in his diary that 'discourse in the street is of death, and nothing else, and few people going up and down, that the towne is like a place distressed and forsaken.' Although it isn't recorded, the likelihood is that Lord and Lady St John, together with their children – the

Chapter Six

The Great Riddle of the Age

Tension had been building between the English and Dutch merchants who fought over the lucrative trade routes for spices, tea, sugar and tobacco. In March 1665, this spilled over into full-blown hostilities with the Second Anglo-Dutch War, which was fought at sea. James, Duke of York commanded the English navy with his uncle, Prince Rupert as vice admiral; the admirals of the three squadrons – the Red, the White and the Blue – were the Duke of York, Prince Rupert and Lord St John's next-door neighbour Edward Montagu, Earl of Sandwich respectively.

On 13 June 1665, a bright summer day, the Dutch fleet attacked; the action, fought 40 miles off the Suffolk coast, became known as the Battle of Lowestoft. The sound of cannon fire could be heard in the plague-ridden streets of London and was a distraction from the daily reports of the spread of the disease. News of the English victory brought some cheer, but the bloody carnage of a seventeenth-century naval battle had taken its toll. The Duke of York had received a close call when a cannonball only just missed him; his three comrades, all close friends who had been standing next to him, took the full force of the shot, as Samuel Pepys recorded in his diary: 'The Earl of Falmouth, Muskerry, and Mr Richard Boyle killed on board the Duke's ship, the *Royall [sic] Charles*, with one shot: their blood and brains flying in the Duke's face; and the head of Mr Boyle striking down the Duke, as some say.'[1]

The king and Henrietta Maria were horrified at the duke's near miss, which came so soon after the deaths of his siblings Henry, Duke of Gloucester and Mary, Princess of Orange. He was the heir to the throne while the queen remained childless, and the duke's mother and elder brother conspired to keep him away from the scene of any action. The Earl of Sandwich took command of the fleet at sea, but was soon relieved of his command when it was suspected that he had been helping himself to more prize money from captured ships than he was entitled to. Into the breach stepped the old warhorse General Monck, now the Duke of Albemarle. Prince Rupert had refused to share

James, Duke of York. (*New York Public Library*)

command with Sandwich, but he held no such qualms about accepting the position alongside Albermarle, whom he respected.

The Dutch fleet licked their wounds during the following winter and rebuilt their ships. Now better armed than their English opponents, the Dutch proved

Edward Montagu, 1st Earl of Sandwich by Sir Peter Lely. (*Yale Center for British Art, Paul Mellon Collection*)

Episode from the Four Days' Naval Battle, 1-4 June 1666, attributed to Willem van de Velde. (*Rijksmuseum*)

more than a match when the two fleets once again confronted each other in what was to become one of the longest naval battles ever fought. The Four Days' Battle, lasting from 1 to 4 June 1666, took place in the Downs. In a hard-fought engagement, the Dutch emerged victorious but both sides suffered heavy losses.

Many miles away from the scene of the action, Lady St John was resident in North Yorkshire, enjoying the cool tranquillity of the countryside during another long, hot summer. In mid-August a second son was born; named William, he was baptized four days later in the parish church at Wensley. Two weeks later, in the early hours of Sunday, 2 September, a fire broke out in a bakery in Pudding Lane, off Eastcheap in the City of London, while the good citizens of the city slept. In the cramped lanes of overhanging wooden buildings, the flames leaped with ferocity from each tinder-dry house to its neighbour, and by mid-morning it was clear that a disaster on an epic and almost unprecedented scale was unfolding. The king and the Duke of York sailed down the Thames from Whitehall, rolled up their sleeves and joined the rescue effort. People battled to save whatever belongings they could, loading them onto carts and boats before trying to negotiate the crush of panicked Londoners heading out of the city, either on foot or via the river. Samuel Pepys, who remained in London, witnessed the fire at first-hand:

The Great Fire of London, with Ludgate and Old Saint Paul's. (*Yale Center for British Art, Paul Mellon Collection*)

Everybody endeavouring to remove their goods and flinging into the river or bringing them into lighters that layoff; poor people staying in their houses as long as till the very fire touched them, and then running into boats, or clambering from one pair of stairs by the water-side to another. And among other things, the poor pigeons, I perceive, were loath to leave their houses, but hovered about the windows and balconys till they were, some of them burned, their wings, and fell down.

That evening, Pepys and his household packed up their valuables. Iron chests full of money were stored in the cellar where it was hoped they would be safe and – famously – a couple of days later Pepys buried his wine and a parmesan cheese in his garden.[2]

The fire raged until the Wednesday, fanned by strong winds and with the thick smoke blocking out the sun so that it was dark as night in the middle of the day. At last the flames were halted by firebreaks, which took effect as the wind dropped. To its western extremity, the inferno stopped at Fetter Lane, less than half a mile away from Lincoln's Inn Fields. Winchester House had escaped the devastation, but it had been a close-run thing.

Fatherhood had done nothing to quell St John's hot-headedness. He was, St John admitted, in a passion when he caused a huge hullaballoo by pulling the

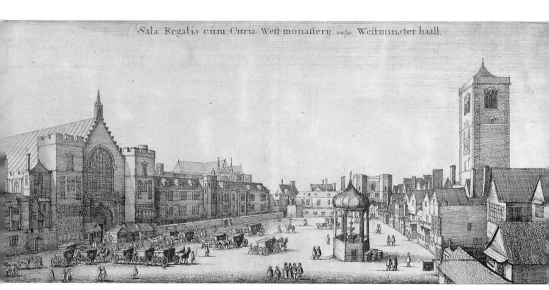

View of New Palace Yard, with Westminster Hall on the left, by Wenceslaus Hollar, 1647. (*Minneapolis Institute of Art*)

nose of a fellow Hampshire landowner in Westminster Hall, 'while the judges were upon their benches' and the court within was in session. Sir Andrew Henley, St John's victim, responded by whacking his opponent over the head with his cane.

The cause of the argument remains unknown but Henley was as bad-tempered as St John. He was the extravagant eldest son of Sir Robert Henley of Bramshill House, a magnificent new mansion built on an ambitious scale. A dispute with the local vicar of neighbouring Eversley Church over the payment of tithes had resulted in the clergyman mounting a thinly-veiled attack on Sir Andrew during a sermon in which he railed against the sin of gluttony; the whole congregation knew that it was a reference to the French chef employed by Henley.[3]

Samuel Pepys, in his diary, made no secret of his dislike of St John and came down firmly on Henley's side of the argument (whatever that argument might have been), sorry only that Henley had retaliated as otherwise all the blame – and the punishment – would have landed on St John's shoulders: '… the judges, they say, will make a great matter: men are only sorry the gentle man did proceed to return a blow; for, otherwise, my Lord would have been soundly fined for the affront, and may be yet for his affront to the judges.'[4]

In the event, it was Henley who came off worse in the eyes of the law. He was imprisoned and charged with *coram rege*, an archaic term denoting that the assault took place, in theory, in the presence of the king himself as the King's Bench court was in his name. St John escaped but later admitted his offence, owning up to being the aggressor and submitting a petition to the king, begging his forgiveness. The king hummed and hawed, but after they had stewed for some time, he pardoned the pair of them (although the whole debacle rumbled on through the courts for some time afterwards).

The misfortunes that beset Charles II's early reign had not yet run their course. The English navy began 1667 in disarray, almost bankrupt and with few options when Parliament refused to allow the king's request for extra funding. By late spring, all the heavy ships of the fleet, the bulk of the navy, were laid up at Chatham with just a small squadron at sea to deter the Dutch. The British fleet was almost defenceless when the Dutch sailed up the Medway towards them in a daring raid. Three of the key English ships – the *Royal James*, the *Royal Oak* and the *Loyal London* – were set ablaze and the flagship, the *Royal Charles*, which had carried the king back from his exile seven years earlier, was captured. Pepys, who was employed as a naval administrator by the Admiralty, was at the forefront of the panic. He recorded the fears of the country: the

Samuel Pepys by John Riley.
(*Yale University Art Gallery*)

French were rumoured to be mustering at Dunkirk (once held by the English, Charles II sold the town back to France in 1662 to replenish his treasury), and a full-blown invasion was feared, with combined Dutch and French forces plotting to overrun the country. The Earl of Clarendon's London home was attacked, the windows smashed, trees felled and a gibbet set up. Upon his gate was written: 'Three sights to be seen; Dunkirke, Tangier, and a barren Queene'. Edward Hyde's position as Lord Chancellor was perilous. Hated across the country, he was suspected of having engineered the marriage between the king and Catherine of Braganza, knowing the queen would not bear a child and leave his grandchildren in line to inherit the crown.

A fragile peace was negotiated that lasted almost five years until, in April 1672, England joined France in declaring war upon the Dutch (the Third Anglo-Dutch War). During the indecisive Battle of Solebay, Edward Montagu, 1st Earl of Sandwich lost his life on board his flagship, HMS *Royal James*. Afterwards talks for peace began anew, with Charles II throwing his weight behind his nephew William of Orange's rights to be *Stadtholder* of Holland. In turn, William filled his uncle's royal coffers with millions of Dutch guilders, although the arguments and battles rumbled on for some time. It kept

Burning of the English Fleet near Chatham, 19-24 June 1667 by Willem Schellinks. (*Rijksmuseum*)

Parliament happy; they were always frightened at the thought of the king being an ally of France, seeing Catholic plots everywhere.[5]

At long last, St John got a form of reward for his loyalty when he was granted several key posts, in particular that of Lord Lieutenant of Hampshire. In early September 1669, St John entertained the king when he visited Southampton together with Prince Rupert of the Rhine and the party amused themselves by hunting in the New Forest and sailing in the Solent. It was reported that Southampton's 'conduits ran with wine' on the occasion. As a Hampshire landowner, and because the family's title was Marquess of Winchester, there was nowhere more suitable for St John's sons' education than Winchester College, one of the oldest public schools in the country. The two boys attended in the mid-1670s as fee-paying commoners, meaning that they were private pupils of the headmaster.[6]

Naval Battle between Michiel Adriaensz de Ruyter and the Duke of York on the *Royal Prince*, 7 June 1672 by Willem van de Velde. (*Rijksmuseum*)

The aging Prince Rupert was now more statesman than military hero. The king appointed him Constable of Windsor Castle, and there Rupert set to with gusto, implementing a comprehensive series of improvements for both practical and pleasurable reasons. Included in the latter were projects close to Rupert's heart. The building of a real tennis court (the sport was a favourite of both the king and Rupert; in Pepys' opinion, Rupert was the 'fourth best tennis player in England') was a priority, as was the provision of apartments within the castle for the woman who had claimed Rupert's heart. She was the actress Margaret (Peg) Hughes, a woman who was 'mighty fine, and pretty' but immodest, according to the old gossip Pepys. An inveterate bachelor, Rupert had denied the claims of his former mistress Frances Bard when, in an echo of the rumours surrounding Charles II and Lucy Walter, Frances told anyone who would listen that Rupert had secretly married her. Frances had given birth to a son named Dudley Bard (also known as Dudley Rupert) and while Rupert looked after Frances and their child, his attention was focused elsewhere.[7]

Frances Bard by Sir Peter Lely. (*Jan Arkesteijn/Wikimedia Commons/PD-US/CC-BY-SA-3.0*)

The court had decamped to Tunbridge Wells so the queen could 'take the waters', hoping that it might help her to conceive a child. Keen to find a diversion that would distract the king from his pursuit of *la belle Stuart*, Catherine of Braganza asked a company of actors to attend. Predictably, the female members of the troupe soon caught the eyes of the king and his companions. The old

Ruperta Howe and Emanuel Scrope Howe. (*Illustrations from* A Collection of Royal Letters *by Sir George Bromley, 1787*)

warhorse Prince Rupert fell head-over-heels for Peg Hughes and, for the king, it was his first glimpse of a woman who would become synonymous with his name. Gaining a reputation for herself on the stage was a young woman named Eleanor – or Nell – Gwyn.

Both Peg and Nell were given rooms in Windsor Castle, as was Peg's brother who was employed within Rupert's household. In 1670, Peg's loyal brother was said to have fought a duel with one of the king's servants after an argument over who was the handsomest woman then living at Windsor, Nell or his sister. Rupert had no doubts over the matter: he was besotted by Peg, even more so when, in 1673, she gave him a daughter, Ruperta. This daughter would grow up to have a close connection to the Powlett family. When Ruperta was 22 years of age, she married Lieutenant General Emanuel Scrope Howe, a grandson of Emanuel Scrope, 1st Earl of Sunderland and Martha Janes (via their daughter Annabella's marriage to John Grubham Howe), making Ruperta niece-by-marriage to St John.

'Pretty, witty Nell', as Pepys dubbed her, grew up in Coal Yard Alley off Drury Lane in London's Covent Garden with an alcoholic mother who kept a local brothel and a wayward sister named Rose. Madame Gwyn, Nell's mother, fell into a ditch one night while drunk and drowned. It wasn't an auspicious start in life for a woman who claimed the heart of a king. Perhaps because of his years spent in a poverty-stricken exile, struggling to make ends meet in royal courts, Charles II was a curious mix of haughty monarch and man of the people. The king adored Nell and was unperturbed by her background, and his subjects loved him all the more for it.

Growing up so close to the theatre in Drury Lane, Nell and her sister Rose worked as orange-girls within the theatre, selling sweet China oranges to the audience for sixpence each. The occupation was seen as an easy stepping-stone to the professions of both actress and whore. Nell chose the former, although she wasn't above calling herself 'the Protestant Whore' when years later she was mobbed in her carriage by an angry crowd who mistook Nell for the king's new French mistress. Nell gave the king two sons and received gifts in the form of houses, jewels and money, but no title. While Barbara Villiers was created the Countess of Castlemaine and later Duchess of Cleveland in her own right, and Louise de Kérouaille (the 'Catholic Whore' to Nell's Protestant one, Louise was introduced to the king by his sister Minette) was rewarded with the title of Duchess of Portsmouth, poor Nell was left with no more name than the one she was given at birth. Her two sons, however, were given Beauclerk as a surname and raised to the peerage (the elder, Charles, became the 1st Duke of St Albans).

By the end of the 1660s, the aged John, Marquess of Winchester had made a third marriage to another Catholic heiress, Isabella, daughter of William Howard, 1st Viscount Stafford. Lord Stafford had survived the tumult of the Civil Wars just to lose his head in the 'Popish Plot', a fictitious conspiracy instigated by Titus Oates who whipped the country into a frenzy in the belief that there was a Catholic conspiracy to assassinate Charles II. By the time of the Popish Plot, however, the brave and loyal 5th Marquess of Winchester was no more. His eldest son Charles, Lord St John succeeded him in the title and gained control of the estates that went with it but precious little else. In his father's will he was barely mentioned: 'I give to my son Charles, Lord St John my Parliament robes.' The marquess had stipulated that mourning be provided for his marchioness and three of his children, Lord Francis and Lady Frances Powlett and Lady Anne Belasyse. Perhaps he knew that he would not be much mourned by his eldest son? Englefield remained the home of the marquess's third wife, and after her it would pass to Charles's younger brother, Lord Francis Powlett. In an echo of his sister-in-law's history, Lord Francis Powlett is said to have secretly married his kitchen maid Anne Breamore (from nearby Tidmarsh). An apocryphal story relating to Francis claims that even the other household servants were kept in the dark. Anne had made a pig's

Eleanor 'Nell' Gwyn, engraving of the portrait by Sir Peter Lely. (*Stanford University Libraries: Leon Kolb collection*)

ear of carving the meat for dinner and the servant whose job it was to serve it complained. He asked Lord Francis whom he should say was responsible and probably wasn't expecting the reply he got back from his master: 'You can tell them that Lady Francis Powlett carved the meat.'[8]

Louise de Kérouaille, Duchess of Portsmouth by Sir Peter Lely. (*Getty Open Content*)

Charles, now the 6th Marquess of Winchester (we'll now refer to him as Winchester rather than St John) commenced building a new mansion in North Yorkshire, the money for this provided by his wife Mary. Bolton Castle was too far destroyed to be rescued and was left a romantic ruin and so, during the

Engraving of Bolton Hall, 1808. (*Authors' own collection*)

1670s, work started on Bolton Hall, some 3 or 4 miles away on the edge of the village of Wensley.

The heady days of the Restoration were at an end. With morale at an all-time low and the coffers empty, Charles II looked to make peace, not war. Winchester, a complex man, still trod a difficult tightrope as he negotiated the politics of the era. Quick to anger, he also affected an eccentricity that seems designed to keep his peers uncertain of his actions and motives. The truth is that his past had probably affected him deeply; as a child he had witnessed the imprisonment and downfall of his father, the destruction of his home and prospects, and been taken from his family. Forced to change his religion, Winchester then negotiated the turbulent Protectorate while staying loyal to the Stuart family and might have expected high rewards at the Restoration. By and large, these rewards still didn't appear, even after he became the 6th

Bolton Castle, from *Antiquities of England and Wales* by Francis Grose, 1785.

Marquess of Winchester. In 1679 there was a rumour that Charles II would elevate Winchester from a marquess to a duke, but it never came to pass. The king was growing old and still had no legitimate children; his heir remained the Catholic James, Duke of York. Winchester, a Protestant and no sycophantic courtier, knew he could expect no favours in the next reign.[9]

On 10 July 1679, at 18 years of age, the marquess's eldest son Charles Powlett (known by his father's lesser title of Earl of Wiltshire rather than Baron St John) married Margaret, daughter of George Coventry, 3rd Baron Coventry. The bride was around three years older than her new husband and Margaret, whose mother was a daughter of the Earl of Thanet, came to the marriage with an eye-watering dowry of 30,000*l*. No expense was spared on the grand wedding which culminated in a ball at Coventry's house where the king was guest of honour. Less than two years later, Margaret was dead and her brother John, who inherited the Coventry estates – and debts – struggled to pay the money still owed to the Powlett family. A year and a day after Margaret's death (after the obligatory twelve months of mourning), the Earl of Wiltshire married again.[10]

His second wife was so well-connected to his own ancestry it is impossible not to suspect that Wiltshire's father instigated the match. Frances Ramsden was

Wensley Church and Bridge from *Antiquities of England and Wales* by Francis Grose, 1785.

one of the five daughters of William Ramsden and his wife Elizabeth, daughter of George Palmes of Naburn Hall on the outskirts of York (a Catholic family). The Ramsdens were a family with a strong Yorkshire heritage: their estates included Byram near Pontefract and Longley Hall at Huddersfield, a Tudor mansion. The family were also hardened Royalists; William Ramsden's father had died in the king's service at Newark Castle during the Civil Wars. There was an even closer link between the two families: William Ramsden's mother was Margaret Frescheville whose niece, Christian, had been Lord Winchester's short-lived first wife. If Winchester still had one eye on filling the coffers of his family with the Frescheville wealth, he was too late. Sir John Frescheville had died a year earlier beset by debts, and Staveley Hall in Derbyshire had been sold off (to William Cavendish, 3rd Earl of Devonshire).[11]

The Ramsden family was coping with the fluctuating fortunes of the era better than the Freschevilles. Besides his five daughters, William Ramsden had three sons, John, Frescheville and Peter; John, the eldest, would later be created a baron. The joint Yorkshire interests of the two families, Ramsden and Powlett, would increase the influence of all concerned in the north of the country.

Mary, Marchioness of Winchester had not lived long enough to witness her son's second marriage. In growing ill-health, Lady Winchester travelled to mainland Europe with her husband to spend the winter in a warmer climate. Heading for the south of France, they reached the ancient town of Moulins on 1 November 1680 and it was there that Mary died. Charles had loved her and was distraught, transporting his wife's body back via Paris to Calais and across the English Channel. Once back in England, he refused to head for Old Basing Church in Hampshire where so many of his ancestors lay; instead he took Mary's body back to North Yorkshire where she had felt most at home, to the small churchyard at Wensley Church.[12]

Without Mary's steadying hand, and perhaps drinking heavily in an attempt to ignore the gulf left in his life by her absence, Winchester grew erratic in his behaviour. Two men who knew the marquess well described his personality and lifestyle in the late 1600s, and they are too similar to be discounted as mere gossip. Gilbert Burnet, later the Bishop of Salisbury, who thought Winchester a 'very knowing and a very crafty politic man', said of him that

> He [Powlett] was a man of a strange mixture. He had the spleen to a high degree and affected an extravagant behaviour; for many weeks he would not open his mouth till such an hour of the day when he thought the air was pure. He changed the day into night, and often hunted by torch-light, and took all sorts of liberties to himself, many of which were very disagreeable to those about him. He was a man of most profuse expense, and of a most ravenous avarice to support that; and tho' he was much hated, yet he carried matters before him with such authority and success, that he was in all respects the great riddle of the age.

A more sympathetic picture was given by a fellow Yorkshireman, Sir John Reresby. Like the Powletts, Sir John was a Royalist. After the Civil Wars he had left England for self-imposed exile abroad and became a trusted confidante of the widowed Henrietta Maria.

In the midst of the impending dangers which seemed to threaten us, there was a nobleman, the Marquis of Winchester, who had, by his conduct, persuaded some people to think him mad, though he certainly acted upon principles of great human prudence. This gentleman passing through Yorkshire on his way to London, I went to pay him a visit; he had four coaches and a hundred horses in his retinue, and staid ten days at a house that he borrowed in our parts. His custom was to dine at six or seven in the evening, and his meal always lasted till six or seven the next morning; during which he sometimes drank; sometimes listened to music; sometimes he fell into discourse; sometimes he took tobacco, and sometimes he ate his victuals; while the company had free choice to sit or rise, to go or come, to sleep or not. The dishes and bottles were all the time before them on the table; and when it was morning, he would hunt or hawk, if the weather was fair; if not, he would dance, go to bed at eleven and repose himself till the evening. Notwithstanding this irregularity, he was a man of great sense, and though, as I just now said, some took him for mad, it is certain his meaning was to keep himself out of the way of more serious censure in these ticklish days, and preserve his estate, which he took great care of.[13]

Winchester had borrowed Rufford Abbey, a former Cistercian abbey in north Nottinghamshire, for ten days to break his journey and it was there Reresby planned to visit his friend, but he arrived a day late and the marquess, with his retinue, was already heading northwards. The abbey, as Reresby observed to its owner, George Savile, 1st Marquess of Halifax, had been left dirtier after Winchester's ten days of occupation than it would be after a year's residence by Lord Halifax's family.

Events in the not too distant future would reveal Gilbert Burnet, Sir John Reresby and the Marquess of Winchester were all treading a dangerous path during the 'ticklish days' of the 1680s. It is almost certain that, at the time Reresby was writing, Winchester was already in secret negotiations with Prince William of Orange, Charles II's Dutch nephew, a perilous – even treasonous – undertaking. The wily marquess's pretended eccentricity was a clever disguise behind which he could hide, and it proved a very successful distraction.

Chapter Seven

Glorious Revolution

James, Duke of York converted to Catholicism after the Restoration, although he tried to keep it secret for a time. Many blamed his wife Anne Hyde's influence. Pretty much straight after her shotgun marriage to the duke, she renounced her Protestant faith in favour of the old religion but, for many years, James paid lip service to the faith of his birth. He attended Anglican services while the country looked askance at the heir to the throne and worried that divisions along religious lines would once more pull the country apart. Charles II took a pragmatic approach to his brother's secret conversion and simply ordered that his two nieces, Mary and Anne, be brought up as Protestants. Public concern led to a period known as the Exclusion Crisis (from 1679 to 1681), when several bills were introduced to the House of Commons in an attempt to bar the Duke of York from succeeding to the throne. These bills were instigated by the Marquess of Winchester's ally, Anthony Ashley Cooper, 1st Earl of Shaftesbury and seconded by another Hampshire MP (and friend of Lord Winchester), Lord William Russell (a younger son of the 5th Earl (later 1st Duke) of Bedford; Russell's Hampshire connection came through his wife who was daughter and co-heiress of Thomas Wriothesley, 4th Earl of Southampton). Although Winchester's name was not mentioned, it is hard to imagine that he wasn't somehow involved in this plan to exclude the Duke of York from ever becoming king. It seems that Charles II was of the same mind and did suspect the Marquess of Winchester. The king dissolved Parliament before any resolution could be passed and turned his back on those men who had supported the bills, including Winchester who was dismissed from his posts as lord lieutenant and *custos rotulorum* (keeper of the rolls) of Hampshire. He would remain out of favour for the rest of Charles II's reign and could expect no favourable treatment in the next, either. Shunned at court, Winchester retreated to his estates. He had concentrated on building Bolton Hall in North Yorkshire; now he turned his attention southwards and commenced building a mansion at Winslade in Hampshire, turning what

Charles Powlett, 6th Marquess of Winchester, later 1st Duke of Bolton. (*Stanford University Libraries: Leon Kolb collection*)

had been a hunting lodge near Basing House into an impressive new country residence in exquisite landscaped grounds. This mansion, named Hackwood, would become the family's main seat in the south of England, the gentle pastoral surroundings forming a contrast to the rugged yet scenic Yorkshire moors in which Bolton Hall stood.[1]

If Winchester was content to take a back seat in the world of politics, his eldest son Charles, Earl of Wiltshire was all too happy to try to fill his father's shoes. Wiltshire was a Whig to his eyeballs. During March 1682, the earl passed through York while paying a visit to his father's northern estates and was 'mightily followed by the Whiggish party' there. In a bout of chauvinistic thuggery – and probably in consequence of some heavy and riotous drinking during the day – Lord Wiltshire had his servants beat up a civilian, a Mr Senior, who made a remark that Wiltshire and his merry friends perceived as an insult. Mr Senior challenged Wiltshire to a duel but the earl, once he'd sobered up, ignored him. Because of his father's connections and status in the county, Wiltshire held the upper hand in the argument. At a ball given by the Dowager Lady Middleton, Senior was forced 'to cry *peccavi* and beg his lordship's pardon publicly'.[2]

Spending the winter of 1682/3 in Hampshire, the Powletts nevertheless kept a close eye on the royal court in London. Anne, Duchess of York was dead, and the duke did nothing to alleviate the country's concerns about his religion with his second marriage. He chose as his bride a 15-year-old Italian Catholic princess, Mary of Modena and all Parliament's fears of a Papist plot sprang up anew. At country estates, under a veil of strict secrecy, men gathered and talked of ways to counter this perceived threat. One of these cloak-and-dagger meetings took place at Rye House in Hertfordshire. The gentlemen present, beside the owner of the house Richard Rumbold, included Winchester's ally, Lord William Russell, and the king's natural son, James Scott, Duke of Monmouth (who had his eye on the throne, despite his illegitimacy) was implicated in the plot.

Their plan was extreme. On 1 April 1683, the king and his brother, the Duke of York, would pass by Rye House on their way back to London from the races at Newmarket. Hidden in a barn facing the road would be a group of armed men to ambush the entourage and assassinate the royal brothers. The location gave this desperate scheme its name: the Rye House Plot. While not one of the active plotters, the Marquess of Winchester was in on the secret and, by his silence, gave his consent.

Rye House in 1771, showing the barn, from the *Supplement to the Antiquities of England and Wales*.

Fate intervened. A fire broke out in one of Newmarket's stables on the evening of 22 March. Fanned by high winds, a few hours later half the town lay in ashes and the races were cancelled. The royal party was unaware of the impending threat to their lives, and the plotters oblivious to the disaster that had unfolded at Newmarket. As a result, the king and his brother rode past Rye House to the safety of their palace in London well before the plotters had caught up with events, but afterwards news of the treachery leaked out. The plotters and their accomplices were rounded up and put on trial, accused of treason. The Marquess of Winchester retreated with aplomb into his professed eccentricity and escaped the fate that befell his comrades. Eleven men and one woman (Elizabeth Gaunt) were either beheaded or suffered the awful traitor's death of being hung, drawn and quartered (Elizabeth was burned at the stake). More were imprisoned or exiled, and several, including the Duke of Monmouth, escaped abroad for their own safety. William, Lord Russell was sentenced to be beheaded and his execution took place on Lincoln's Inn Fields, in front of Lord Winchester's house. Jack Ketch was the executioner and he botched the job, taking several swings of his axe before he managed to

William, Lord Russell by Gerard Soest. (*Jan Arkesteijn/Wikimedia Commons/PD-US/CC-BY-SA-3.0*)

sever Lord Russell's head from his body. Afterwards, Russell's remains were 'first carried into Lord Marquess Winchester's house, where his head was put on, and from thence in a hearse … to Southampton House'. It was a risky move by Winchester to allow his house to be used, but indicative of his loyalty to his friends. Winchester – wise through his supposed madness – wasn't at home at the time. He had travelled abroad after the failure of the plot, and in a letter to the physician and naturalist Martin Lister, dated 27 April 1683, Winchester begged Lister, who was ill, to journey to France with him, where he was following 'my Lord' to 'stay in some pleasant town'.[3]

By the summer, Winchester was back in England. He sojourned at the seaside town of Scarborough on England's north coast, 'taking the waters' for his health in company with a Scotsman, Robert Murray of Tibbermore near Perth. Murray was a long-standing friend, ostensibly at the marquess's side because he 'was very diverting to me in my weak health and he was very careful of me in my sickness' (Murray had been with Winchester in Hampshire during the preceding winter). At this juncture in time, it's nigh on impossible to say whether the tricky marquess was ill or whether it was just a convenient and difficult to disprove excuse; if the latter, it would not be the first or the last time that Winchester would use his health as a smokescreen to protect him from censure. Either way, the entertaining Murray remained with the marquess all through the summer and then returned to Bolton Hall with him. In the aftermath of the Rye House Plot, someone who clearly had a grudge against both Winchester and Murray turned informant and suggested that Murray was concerned in the matter and was occupied in raising a rebellion in the north of the country. The implication was that Winchester was also embroiled in this scandal.

The authorities in London sent a messenger up to North Yorkshire to apprehend Murray with ambiguous letters to the marquess, politely suggesting that he was innocent of any knowledge about his companion's nefarious activities. Winchester had no option but to let the messenger arrest Murray and take him back to London, but he sent with him a letter asserting Murray's innocence. Murray and a few fellow Scotsmen were rounded up in the investigation and ended up back in Scotland where they were held in custody ahead of a trial. Murray's accuser withdrew his evidence and Winchester wrote to Whitehall to ask for his friend to be freed, but to keep on the right side of the king, made sure to add he would 'give [Murray] no hope of taking him back into service, though very useful to me in my ill health, unless fully assured of his innocence, and that such a step would not be disagreeable to

the King and Duke'. The response to this was a reply from the Secretary of
State, Sir Leoline Jenkins, after Winchester's letter had been read to the king,
the Duke of York and to the Lords; though polite, Jenkins' exasperation with
Winchester was clear, and Winchester understood the inference that the court
had mocked him. Winchester's last epistle on the matter, written from Bolton
Hall to Jenkins, could not have endeared him to the court at all. With faux
subservience, Winchester made his feelings obvious:

> You will hardly believe into what a transport of joy I was carried on
> receipt of yours of the 8th, whereby I was assured not only of his
> Majesty's and his Royal Highness' gracious acceptance of my letter
> relating to Mr Murray, but also of the kind and concurrent advice of
> so many lords of the Council with yourself. I am better able to bear the
> burthen of my broken health and the solitudes of these cold northern
> parts, whilst I have the favourable respects of such friends at Court...[4]

In the years that followed the Rye House Plot, Charles II's health steadily
declined, but it still came as a surprise to everyone when he collapsed at
Whitehall Palace. The king suffered a stroke after spending the night in the
Duchess of Portsmouth's arms and lingered for four days, nursed by the
duchess, but there was no hope of a recovery. Hours before he died, Father
John Huddleston was brought to the king's bedside by the Duke of York;
Father Huddleston had helped Charles to escape after the Battle of Worcester
in 1651 and James presented him to his brother with the words, 'Sire, this good
man once saved your life. He now comes to save your soul.' Huddleston heard
the king's confession and received him, on his deathbed, into the Catholic
Church. As ever with Charles II, his women were on his mind to the last,
in particular Louise de Kérouaille, Duchess of Portsmouth and Nell Gwyn;
he told James to 'be well to Portsmouth and let not poor Nelly starve'. On 6
February 1685, the 54-year-old Charles II died, to be succeeded by his brother
as James II of England and James VII of Scotland.

Despite Parliament's fears, the new Catholic king (not since Henry VIII's
daughter Mary Tudor 132 years earlier had there been a Catholic monarch)
reigned with religious tolerance at first. In fact, in contrast with his past excesses,
the new king wanted his royal court to be a private, moral and frugal one.
Known to have entertained a string of mistresses during both his marriages,
James dispensed with the services of his current paramour, Catherine Sedley.
Courtiers looked on in disbelief and labelled the new king 'Dismal Jimmy'.

Charles II by Jacob Huysmans. (*Royal Pavilion & Museums, Brighton & Hove*)

It didn't last long though, and a few short months later, Catherine was once again by James's side. She was the vivacious, although not conventionally beautiful daughter of the Restoration poet Sir Charles Sedley, MP and had caught James's eye when she danced attendance on Mary of Modena as one of her ladies. The self-deprecating Catherine laughed at the conquest she had

Catherine Sedley, engraving by Richard Tompson. (*Yale Center for British Art, Paul Mellon Collection*)

made: 'It cannot be my beauty for he must see I have none; and it cannot be my wit, for he has not enough to know that I have any.' Catherine was given a life peerage and created the Countess of Dorchester.[5]

The wily old Marquess of Winchester pleaded illness, either real or pretend, to avoid leaving the safety of the relative anonymity he enjoyed at Bolton Hall and going to London for James II's coronation or to the opening of his Parliament. 'Since the notice of the late King's death', he wrote to the Earl of Sunderland, he was 'not able to eat above once in 48 hours and then digest with great pain and difficulty. If I omit any prescribed exercises, I faint.' Winchester's litany of ailments was bladder and kidney stones, indigestion and wind, probably largely self-inflicted by feasting, especially in light of the reports that he presided over riotous dinner tables for twelve hours in succession. In the same letter to Sunderland, Winchester also distanced himself from his eldest son Charles, Earl of Wiltshire, who had clearly been a little less circumspect than his father in airing his views on the new king. 'If my son Wilts[hire] be ungrateful to the King I would not have him stand [for Parliament], because I cannot pass for him, having been for some time a stranger to him.' (The Earl of Wiltshire's daughter Mary had been christened at Wensley a year earlier, so the two had not been strangers for very long.) Winchester made it clear to Sunderland, notwithstanding his ailments, that he would like to be Lord Lieutenant of Hampshire again, if it were possible, despite being ensconced in deepest North Yorkshire. The marquess wasn't prepared to countenance any plans for travel unless he could do so with his great friend, Dr William Mason who had been Wensley's vicar until his retirement. Mason also professed to some kind of medical skill, on which Winchester had come to rely. 'A physician in charity but a divine in practice and the only one [I] can trust with safety to [my] weak health' is how Winchester described Mason. With this man by his side, the marquess ventured to think about travelling south to Hackwood in the summer.[6]

Despite James II's religious tolerance, many in Parliament remained deeply unhappy at the idea of a Catholic king. Plots were being hatched and at the centre of one was the king's nephew. James Scott, Duke of Monmouth, was in self-imposed exile in the Netherlands following the Rye House escapade and in contact with William, Prince of Orange. The prince was now married to James II's daughter, Mary. For years, Charles II had half-hinted that he would make Monmouth his heir, using his son as a pawn in the game between the rival Protestant and Catholic, Whig and Tory factions at court but with no real intention of doing anything so drastic. Monmouth's hopes had been raised, however, and he saw the crown within his grasp. The Prince of Orange knew exactly what Monmouth was up to, and was happy to play a much longer game while turning a blind eye to his cousin's schemes.

By his wife, Monmouth had two children who survived to adulthood and two more by his mistress, the court beauty Eleanor Needham, daughter of Sir Robert Needham, MP. Like Catherine Sedley, Eleanor had been one of Mary of Modena's ladies and that was how she met Monmouth. She gave her lover a son, James, and a daughter, Henrietta, both of whom took Crofts as a surname. Monmouth took care of his second family, setting Eleanor and her children up in a house on Russell Street in Bloomsbury, but his heart lay elsewhere. He had met the woman who would become the love of his life, the heiress Lady Henrietta Wentworth.[7]

Assured of support at home, Monmouth raised money for ships, arms and soldiers (his long-suffering wife and mother-in-law pawned their jewels to help fund the endeavour), and a joint rebellion was raised with Archibald Campbell, Earl of Argyll. Campbell sailed for Scotland and raised his clansmen, while Monmouth headed for the south-west of England, landing at Lyme Regis in Dorset on 11 June 1685. As hoped, men did flock to his side, but not enough. Monmouth had been led to believe that the Marquess of Winchester's eldest son, Lord Wiltshire, would raise the noblemen of Hampshire in support and head towards Lyme Regis. It looks probable that Lord Wiltshire had indeed participated in the secret negotiations surrounding what became known as the Monmouth Rebellion, but in the event he held back from committing himself. He was wise to have done so, although Winchester despaired of his errant son and heir. For a time father and son were at loggerheads. Monmouth headed to Bristol, determined to take the city, but James II had been aware of his nephew's audacious plan for many weeks and was ready with an army that was bearing down on the unsuspecting rebels. Monmouth's ships were captured by the Royal Navy, so retreat was impossible and Argyll's Scottish rebellion failed. Still Monmouth could have seized victory if he had followed through with his plan to take Bristol, but hindsight is a brilliant thing and skirmishes along the way tricked him into believing that the Royalist forces in the area were numerous; in reality, the bulk of the king's army had not yet reached Somerset. Bristol was within Monmouth's grasp, and if he had taken control of that strategic city then his support would have grown and history could have been very different.

Instead, Monmouth veered away and criss-crossed Somerset until he met with the king's main force at what became known as the Battle of Sedgemoor on 6 July. It was an unmitigated defeat for Monmouth and his men. Two days later, the dishevelled duke was discovered hiding in a ditch and taken to London where he was tried, found guilty and sentenced to death as a traitor. Monmouth's pleas for mercy to his uncle the king fell on deaf ears. Jack Ketch again wielded the axe at Monmouth's beheading, this time on Tower Hill. As in the case of William, Lord Russell, the blundering Ketch made a mess of

James Scott, 1st Duke of Monmouth, engraving after Jan Wyck. (*Yale Center for British Art, Paul Mellon Collection*)

his job (estimates vary, but it took between five and eight blows for the axe to cleave Monmouth's head from his body).[8]

The marquess's eldest son, Lord Wiltshire, was the father of a small family; with his second wife the earl had six children, four of whom survived infancy. With the characteristic imaginativeness of the Powletts when it came to naming their offspring, the eldest son carried on the family tradition and was yet another Charles Powlett. He was born at Chawton Manor House in

Hampshire which Lord Wiltshire leased from the owners, the Knight family. (The Knights were later connected by marriage to the family of Jane Austen. Chawton Manor is famous for being the residence of Jane Austen's brother, Edward; Jane herself spent the last years of her life living in a small house on the other side of the village of Chawton, together with her mother and sister, Cassandra.) Conveniently close enough to Basing and Hackwood for Lord Wiltshire to enjoy hunting on his family's estates, Winchester dissembled when it came to allowing his son to live in the mansions he owned, still too raw from his son's escapades in support of the Duke of Monmouth to risk showing much favour. As well as Chawton Manor, the earl and his burgeoning family had a smart London address. Great Queen Street runs between Drury Lane and Lincoln's Inn Fields and it was to this road, one of the most fashionable in London and just around the corner from the family's Arch Row home that the earl moved. His mansion was known as Paulet [Powlett] House and had once been a much larger residence (named Bristol House), but sometime before 1684 when the earl moved in, it had been divided into two properties. It was the eastern half (afterwards Freemasons' Tavern) which formed Paulet House. The young family was still there five years later and during that time, two short-lived sons were born, Scroop (born and christened on the same day, hinting at urgency in the matter) and two years later Thomas, who survived less than a year. Then came Harry, who thrived, and there was also a second daughter, named Frances for her mother.[9]

It might not have been the best time to arrange a marriage, but a match was afoot for Lord Winchester's daughter, Lady Betty. With matters in the country at a fever pitch and courtiers scrambling to stay on the right side of the king's wrath, Lady Betty was proposed as a wife for a man no-one else wanted. Her intended was Robert, Lord Spencer, otherwise known as 'Lewd Rakehelly Spencer', which gives a good insight into his character. Betty's disreputable beau – who didn't seem too keen on the match with a younger daughter of the reclusive and tricky marquess – was a mere 20 years of age and the eldest son and heir of Robert Spencer, 2nd Earl of Sunderland, whose estate, Althorp Hall, lay in Northamptonshire. (While the earldom of Sunderland in its first creation had died with Betty's grandfather, Emanuel Scrope, the title had been resurrected and given to the Spencer family.) The 2nd Earl of Sunderland had been 2 years old when his father died; as an adult, he negotiated the reign of Charles II by cultivating the friendship of the king's French Catholic mistress, Louise de Kérouaille. After the old king's death, Sunderland managed a nimble dance to become one of James II's most trusted aides via the patronage of the

Freemasons' Tavern, Great Queen Street: the central building was once two properties and Paulet House was the one on the left-hand side. (*Leutha/Wikimedia Commons/PD-US/CC-BY-SA-3.0*)

queen, Mary of Modena, and it was in this capacity that the marquess had been writing to Sunderland, excusing his absence in London for James II's coronation. By 1687, both Sunderland and his eldest son were high in favour with the king, flirting with Catholicism and hinting that they may convert. With the Marquess of Winchester at odds with James II and a staunch Protestant to boot, it wasn't just religious matters that perturbed him in regard to Lady Betty's suitor. Even at a young age, the spoiled lad had been heading down the wrong path. When the diarist John Evelyn was approached by Robert's fond mother, the Countess of Sunderland (described by Princess Anne in 1688 as 'the greatest jade that ever was'), asking for Evelyn's help in arranging a marriage between her son and Sir Stephen Fox's daughter Jane, he declined as he was 'afraid [Lord Robert] would prove an extravagant man; for though a youth of extraordinary parts, & that had all the Education imaginable to render him

James II, engraving after Sir Godfrey
Kneller. (*Yale Center for British Art, Paul
Mellon Collection*)

a worthy man; yet his early inclinations to vice made me apprehensive.' The boy's father was a concern for Evelyn too, 'being much sunke in his Estate, by Gaming & other prodigalities'.[10]

Evelyn's concerns about Lord Robert were justified. The young lad assaulted Charles Dormer, 2nd Earl of Carnarvon and was banished abroad, but his temporary exile made no impression on his conduct. He got as far as Switzerland and then, in Geneva, managed to provoke a man named Odet Fabry into challenging him to a duel (rumour suggested that the matter concerned the infidelity of Fabry's beautiful wife). Lord Spencer came off worse (as he always seemed to) and was wounded.

Returning to England, Spencer was beaten up by the watch while 'upon a high ramble' in London with his friends; quite possibly the merry band included Lord Wiltshire, Winchester's eldest son and heir. The Earl of Sunderland, when his son's friends complained to him about the watch's treatment of Lord Robert, wearily shook his head and said 'it was pity it wasn't worse'.[11]

Lord Robert's 'high rambles' might have been overlooked as aristocratic high jinks, but they turned into excursions of a very different nature. In a bizarre turn of affairs, the sleepy market town of Bury St Edmunds in Suffolk had become a hotbed of religious fervour and strife during James II's reign. Because of a charter drawn up by Charles II before his death, the king was able to appoint Bury St Edmunds' mayor and town officials and – crucially – it was only the mayor together with a select few aldermen and citizens who were able to cast a vote in elections. James II abused his royal prerogative to appoint Catholic men to positions of authority within the town so their votes would help to secure a Parliament favourable to the crown. Although Catholics were a minority in Bury St Edmunds, they held all the power and it wasn't long before discontent turned to open rebellion and rioting in the once quiet streets. Enter Robert, Lord Spencer into the town – predictably drunk – in the early spring of 1687. He made for the church and, staggering up the aisle, insulted the parson. It didn't end there. Spencer laid hold of the hapless

cleric and would have dragged him from his pulpit had not the astonished and
irate congregation jumped into action. They stripped the drunken youth, beat
him half senseless and then dragged him through the filthy gutter of Bury St
Edmunds' main street. Although the Earl of Sunderland begged the king to
cashier his loutish son, James II refused to listen, knowing that father and son
were – step by step – converting to the 'old religion'.

While these shenanigans were taking place, Lady Betty Powlett was living
with her brother Charles's family at Chawton Manor in Hampshire; her father
wrote repeatedly to the Earl of Sunderland asking if the marriage was still to
go ahead and tried to establish his daughter's view on the matter. Sunderland
refused to reply, and Winchester took that as proof that he had no control over
Lord Spencer and was ashamed of his son. With what looks like misplaced
indulgence, Winchester declared that if Lady Betty still wanted her rakehell,
then he would allow the marriage to take place and he put money for her dowry
to one side in readiness (the marriage settlement would cost him 17,000*l.* if it
went ahead). Although now reconciled to his eldest son (who was restored to
the favour of both his father and the king), Winchester was at his wit's end as
it wasn't just Lady Betty's forthcoming nuptials that were giving him sleepless
nights. His daughter Mary followed her sister's example and fell prey to a man
who was a cad of the first order. Both young women were in their twenties,
and in an age where it was usual to marry young, they were worried about
ending up as old maids. It seems that the Powlett household was suffering from
the lack of a mother, and their father, with his real or pretended illness, had
allowed them considerable freedom compared to their peers. Mary had been
ill for most of 1686, but when recovered made a secret marriage to a roguish
Yorkshire gentleman, Tobias Jenkins of Grimstone. Rachel, Lady Russell,
who knew the family well, hinted at dark secrets hidden within the union:

> Sir John Talbot is to be made a lord presently: the king says he finds him
> to be a gentleman of better understanding than almost any he knows in
> England, and judges him to be a person of integrity; which is more than
> can be pronounced of Mr Jenkins of the north, heir to an estate of 1200
> pounds per annum.
>
> He was accused as the author of lady Mary Pawlet's grievous
> misfortune, but with great asseverations he denied it to persons of the
> best quality that were concerned for her; yet now owns himself her
> husband more than a year past. Enough of so bad a story.

Whatever the truth of the 'bad story', it was buried in so comprehensive a manner by the family that there is very little record of the discord. When the truth crept out, Winchester and his son Lord Wiltshire strenuously confirmed that Lady Mary was indeed married, contrary to rumour, but letters between father and son reveal their dissatisfaction with the match. Had Lady Mary eloped with her husband, or had a child out of wedlock? She is known to have had two children with Tobias; Elizabeth (who died young) and Mary who was mentioned in her grandfather's will. Poor Lady Mary's marriage, real or otherwise, didn't last many years: she was buried in York Minster (her daughter, Elizabeth, who died almost a year after her mother, lays alongside her).[12]

Winchester's eldest daughter had made a much better match. Back in 1673, Lady Jane Powlett married John Egerton, the future 3rd Earl of Bridgewater, as his second wife. It was a rock-solid and loving union which produced nine healthy children, but tragedy struck the family in April 1687 when the two eldest sons were killed in a fire at their London home, Bridgewater House.

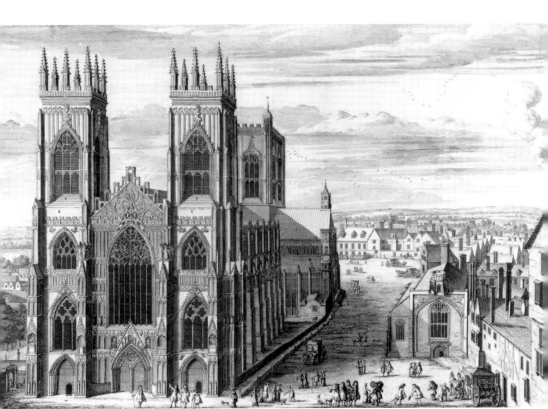

The west end of the Cathedral Church of St Peter in York. (*York Museums Trust*)

The youngsters died along with a servant who caused the conflagration by the 'ill placing of his candle' while putting the boys to bed. Thus, the third son, Scroop Egerton, succeeded his father and, in time, became the 1st Duke of Bridgewater. The Marquess of Winchester was heartbroken at the news of his grandsons' death: while he didn't see too much of his grandchildren, he loved

Jane, Countess of Bridgewater, engraving after Michael Dahl. (*Yale Center for British Art, Paul Mellon Collection*)

to hear about them and always sent his love in his letters. In one letter to his son, Winchester asked to be remembered to 'the little monsters'. For months, Winchester had been looking forward to his eldest son visiting Bolton; Lord Wiltshire was in London, delivering Betty into her sister Jane's safe hands while he travelled north (Betty's proposed marriage was still causing ructions). As soon as the awful news of the fire reached Bolton Hall, Winchester wrote to his son to tell him to stay in London at his sister's side as long as she needed him there and not to think about heading for Bolton for a while.[13]

Following the riot in Bury St Edmunds, James II came up with an ingenious solution to get Robert, Lord Spencer out of everyone's hair for the time being. His mother-in-law's death conveniently gave James the perfect excuse and Lord Spencer was packed off to Italy on behalf of the king and queen to convey their condolences regarding the deceased Duchess of Modena (Laura Martinozzi who died in Rome during July 1687). Robert roistered his way across mainland Europe before falling ill at Turin. There he lay all through the winter that followed, until recovered enough to make it to Paris. Together with the Duke of Norfolk and the British envoy-extraordinary to Paris, Bevil Skelton, Lord Spencer was given a tour of the magnificent gardens at Versailles. Robert's choice of companions was interesting. Skelton was at Versailles because James II feared an attack on his throne from William of Orange, and the British envoy was instructed to make an ally of France. Norfolk, meanwhile, was there because England had become a little too hot to hold him. A Catholic who had paid lip service and conformed to the Church of England for the sake of his estates, he had fallen foul of the king by criticizing James II's policy of stuffing towns such as Bury St Edmunds with Catholic officials. Robert enjoyed the visit to Versailles' gardens and the hospitality on offer. He was presented to Louis XIV and to the French king's daughter-in-law, the *dauphine* Maria Anna Victoria of Bavaria, but was too drunk to make any kind of reply to their courtesies. This was the beginning of the end for Lewd Rakehelly Spencer. His body could take no further abuse and by the summer he was bedridden in his Parisian lodgings. Almost comatose and unable to speak, he died on 25 September, his death attributed either to an excess of brandy or to the wounds he had received in the contretemps at Bury St Edmunds a year and a half earlier, depending on to whom you spoke. Poor Lady Betty had been left in limbo: although her family mounted a search for a suitable replacement husband, Lady Betty was still unmarried in the spring of the following year.[14]

Louis XIV by Hyacinthe
Rigaud. (*Getty Open
Content*)

Lady Betty had to fend for herself. With England becoming too hot to hold them, several aristocratic gentlemen who found themselves at odds with the king felt it prudent to leave the country and many headed for William of Orange's Protestant Court. By the time of Robert, Lord Spencer's death, the Marquess of Winchester had sent both his sons to the prince's side in the Netherlands. It was – at last – a bold move from a man who had hitherto refused to commit himself to one side or another. The Bolton dynasty was now tied to the fortunes of the Prince and Princess of Orange, for better or for worse.

The Earl of Wiltshire's growing nursery, and the secured continuance of the Bolton dynasty, was in direct contrast to the royal court. Mary of Modena had endured no fewer than ten pregnancies, and each one had ended either in miscarriage, stillbirth or a child who died in infancy. Upon James II taking the throne, his heirs remained the two daughters from his first marriage, Mary and Anne. This changed in the early summer of 1688 with the birth of a son on 10 June 1688. Rumours quickly spread that the boy, named James Francis Edward, was not the king's son but a 'changeling' who had been smuggled into Whitehall Palace in a warming pan and substituted for the queen's stillborn child. (The Countess of Sunderland, Robert Spencer's mother, was one of Mary's ladies and present at the birth.)

In 1677 James II's eldest daughter Mary had married – at the instigation of her uncle and largely against the wishes of her father – her cousin, the dour and reserved William, Prince of Orange and had lived in the Netherlands since that time. While the Protestant Mary, Princess of Orange, had been heir to the throne, those who opposed the king's religion had been prepared to bide their time, but now they talked of rebellion, with plans to overthrow the king in favour of his daughter and her husband, the Prince of Orange. English exiles began to gather at William's court, and two of the first to do so (in April 1688 and well before the Prince of Orange had fully committed himself to the cause) were the Marquess of Winchester's sons, the Earl of Wiltshire and Lord William Powlett, sent there at their father's express command. The Marquess of Winchester, meanwhile, remained in the north of England and 'was forc'd, like *Brutus*, to act the part of Lunacy, which he could indeed do the better, for that with all his good Sense, he was the most extravagant Humourist in *Britain*.' His good friend Anthony Ashley Cooper, Earl of Shaftesbury, alone wasted no time in raising 40,000*l*. for the swiftly-organized expedition. When the invasion fleet landed in November 1688 at Torbay in Devon, the Powlett brothers were by William's side as he stepped ashore and began his march inland in wet and windy weather typical of England, negotiating mud and floods while keeping an eye open for James II's expected troops. The latter failed to materialize in the West Country. On 9 November William took Exeter and a few days later appointed Lord Wiltshire as his revenue commissioner. As the Prince of Orange's forces continued towards London, it took just one battle, at Reading, to defeat the king who, with his wife and son, fled into exile.

William III, Prince of Orange, portrait in the manner of Willem Wissing. (*Rijksmuseum*)

Mary II after Sir Godfrey Kneller. (*Yale Center for British Art, Paul Mellon Collection*)

The following year, after William threatened to withdraw his troops, Parliament was persuaded to make William and Mary joint monarchs. It was the Marquess of Winchester who tabled a motion to Parliament asking the House to appoint the couple as co-rulers. Afterwards, the rebellion became known as the Glorious Revolution and for the fortunes of the Powletts, who had been so instrumental in its success, it lived up to its name. Two days before William and Mary's coronation, the Marquess of Winchester was created the 1st Duke of Bolton and regained his positions as lord lieutenant and *custos rotulorum* of Hampshire. He was also made warden of the New Forest. It was more reward than Charles II had ever bestowed on the family, despite the Powletts' loyalty to the Stuart cause. At the coronation in Westminster Abbey, the new duke carried the queen's orb, and his daughter, Lady Betty, the queen's train.[15]

The Earl of Wiltshire, after his father became a duke, took the lesser peerage as his courtesy title and became the 7th Marquess of Winchester (and so henceforth we shall now refer to him as Winchester for the rest of his father's lifetime). Both Lord and Lady Winchester were given positions at court within the inner circle of the monarchy: the marquess was made Lord Chamberlain of the royal household and the marchioness one of Mary II's ladies of the bedchamber.

Jacobite uprisings in favour of the deposed James II continued in Ireland and Scotland. Ireland was a Catholic country and vociferously resisted having a Protestant king and queen foisted upon it, so William had little choice but to quell the dissent by force and James saw one last chance to regain his crown. In growing desperation, the deposed monarch landed in Ireland with an army. James' and William's forces met at the Battle of the Boyne (at Oldbridge, County Meath), where James was defeated once and for all. He fled back to France and never set foot on British soil again. James did, however, make a

The Battle of the Boyne by Jan van Huchtenburg. (*Rijksmuseum*)

declaration, reaffirming his and his infant son's right to rule, at the end of which he promised to pardon everyone involved in overthrowing him, however guilty, except for a few notable exceptions. Charles Powlett, Marquess of Winchester was the second name on the list of those who would not be pardoned (the deposed James II choosing not to recognize Powlett's dukedom); the duke's eldest son was also included in this list (as Lord Wiltshire).[16]

The Duke of Bolton was left in no doubt that if the Stuart dynasty was to ever regain the British throne, then the ensuing witch hunt would be reminiscent of the one carried out by Charles II when he took vengeance on his father's regicides … and would place both the duke and his sons in peril of their lives. Their fates depended on the continuance of William and Mary's Protestant monarchy.

To the duke's consternation, the ruling dynasty looked somewhat shaky and had a distinct shortage of direct heirs. William III and Mary II ruled jointly for five years until Mary's death from smallpox. They had no children but, under the terms of the Bill of Rights which had confirmed his succession to the throne, William ruled independently for the rest of his life. Next in line after William was Mary's sister Anne, the wife of Prince George of Denmark. At the time of Mary's death, Anne had already been pregnant eleven times. In a situation reminiscent of the experiences of her stepmother, Mary of Modena, all but three of Anne's pregnancies had resulted in miscarriage, stillbirth or children who died within hours of their births. Just three children survived for any length of time, and of these the two eldest, both daughters, died young after contracting smallpox. Anne's one living child was a sickly boy, Prince William, Duke of Gloucester, born almost nine months after the Glorious Revolution. The hopes of the country rested on his shoulders.

without the approbation of the Duke of Bolton. One of Sir Joseph Williamson, MP's correspondents wrote on 10 August 1697 to say:

> It is confidently reported … that Lord Winchester, going over with fine Mrs Crofts, has fallen in love with her and married her in Dublin, she being certainly the blazing star of that kingdom. I never inquired after her fortune, nor I believe did Lord Winchester.

News of the marriage wasn't made public until October and, with a monumental understatement, it was revealed that the duke was 'not a little displeased' with his eldest son. The king intervened, however, on behalf of a lady with such close connections to the royal family, and the following month the duke wrote to Winchester – through gritted teeth – to say that he forgave him 'as the King has commanded me'. Winchester and Henrietta had one son and his name was given in an attempt to distance Henrietta from her father's failed rebellion against the crown and to ingratiate her with William III. He was christened with the unusual forename of Nassau, which recognized his father's loyalty to his monarch and referenced the Dutch royal house of Orange-Nassau. The Duke of Bolton made the best of the situation and mended bridges with his son and new daughter-in-law. Two years later, with the sudden death of Charles Powlett, 1st Duke of Bolton while on a visit to a relative (Norton Powlett of Amport House near Andover), Charles, Lord Winchester became the 2nd Duke of Bolton and Henrietta his duchess. (We shall now refer to the 7th Marquess of Winchester as the duke or simply Bolton; the 2nd duke's eldest son, another Charles Powlett, took the courtesy title of 8th Marquess of Winchester.)[5]

While William III had benefitted from the Powlett family's support and counted them among his greatest allies, relationships between the new duke and the rest of the royal family were not so cordial. The 2nd Duke of Bolton was jealous of the influence that John Churchill, Earl (and later Duke) of Marlborough wielded over Princess Anne, and Bolton's marriage to Henrietta Crofts, the princess's cousin, gained him no ascendancy in Anne's personal sphere. In the thick of all the court intrigues, the Duke of Marlborough had enjoyed love affairs with both Charles II's and James II's discarded mistresses (Barbara, Duchess of Cleveland and Catherine Sedley), but when he had married – in secret, during the winter of 1677/78 – he chose Sarah Jennings, co-heir (with her sister) of a Hertfordshire estate and maid of honour to Mary of Modena when she was Duchess of York. Sarah was also great friends with the duchess's step-daughter Princess Anne and the two women grew close;

Henrietta Crofts, after Sir Godfrey Kneller. (*Yale Center for British Art, Paul Mellon Collection*)

they famously referred to each other as Mrs Morley (Anne) and Mrs Freeman (Sarah). Sarah came to exert almost complete control over Anne's life, indispensable to the princess. The Marlboroughs' influence over the woman who was heir to the throne was therefore all-encompassing and Bolton could not hope to compete; Henrietta was disapproved of at court, and her elevation to the peerage made scant difference to anything. Bolton made little secret of his increasing dislike for Princess Anne, even possibly going so far as to embark upon a proposed plot that had the aim of bypassing Anne and offering the throne to her relation, Sophia of Hanover. In retaliation, Anne made several cruel jibes about him that influenced public opinion, leaving us with the unflattering descriptions of the 2nd Duke of Bolton which are still repeated today: a great booby and a lewd, vicious man.

When William III died in 1702 – after a short illness brought on from complications following a broken collarbone when the king's horse stumbled on a molehill – the crown passed to his sister-in-law, who ruled as Queen Anne (her husband, Prince George of Denmark was her consort, not a co-ruler). The change of monarch was clearly not without its difficulties for the Duke of Bolton for neither he nor his wife was in high favour.

By the time Anne came to the throne, her one surviving child, William, Duke of Gloucester, who had never been strong, had died. The queen had no direct heirs and the succession once more hung in the balance. Some looked to Anne's Catholic half-brother, James Francis Edward Stuart (James II having died in exile in 1701), who was self-proclaimed as James III of England and Ireland (and James VIII of Scotland). Louis XIV of France offered his support to the Jacobite claim and for several years afterwards, Jacobites drank the health of the 'little gentleman in black velvet', the mole who was responsible for the molehill upon which William's horse lost his footing.

Miniature of Queen Anne by Charles Boit. (*Rijksmuseum*)

Charles Powlett, 5th Duke of Bolton.

George III by Allan Ramsay. (*Indianapolis Museum of Art*)

John Powlett, 5th Marquess of Winchester. (*New York Public Library*)

Jane, Countess of Winchester by Gilbert Jackson. (*PKM/Wikimedia Commons/PD-US/ CC-BY-SA-3.0*)

Charles I and his family, by Remi Van Leemput. (*Birmingham Museum*)

Emanuel Scrope, 1st Earl of Sunderland.

Rupert of the Rhine, after Anthony van Dyck. (*Rijksmuseum*)

Charles II while in exile, 1653, by Philippe de Champaigne. (*Cleveland Art Museum*)

Barbara Villiers, studio of Sir Peter Lely. (*National Gallery of Art*)

Mary, Princess of Orange, widow of William II by Bartholomeus van der Helst. (*Rijksmuseum*)

Anne Hyde, by Nicholas Dixon. (*Cleveland Art Museum*)

Mary of Modena, by Willem Wissing. (*Yale Center for British Art, Paul Mellon Collection*)

Charles Powlett, 1st Duke of Bolton.
(*JimmyJoe87/Wikimedia Commons/PD-US/*
CC-BY-SA-3.0)

Mary II when Princess of Orange, by Caspar
Netscher. (*Rijksmuseum*)

William III, by Godfried Schalcken.
(*Rijksmuseum*)

Charles Powlett, 2nd Duke of Bolton.

Lavinia Fenton.

George I, by Sir Godfrey Kneller. (*Yale Art Gallery*)

The Beggars' Banquet by William Hogarth. (*Yale Center for British Art, Paul Mellon Collection*)

Winchester College by Barfoot, 1692 (the gentleman commoners lodged to the right of the centre tower). (*Winchester College*)

Frederick, Prince of Wales, by Charles Philips. (*Yale Center for British Art, Paul Mellon Collection*)

Sir Joseph Banks by Joyce Aris, after Sir Joshua Reynolds. (*Te Papa*)

Jean Mary Brown Powlett, later Lady Bolton.

Admiral Harry Powlett, 6th Duke of Bolton, by Francis Cotes. (*Metropolitan Museum of Art*)

Katherine Lowther. (*Library and Archives of Canada*)

FIDELITY

Katherine Powlett, daughter of the 6th Duke of Bolton by Daniel Gardner. (*From 1921 book on Gardner by Dr G.C. Williamson*)

Queen Charlotte, by Georg David Matthieu. (*Nationalmuseum, Sweden*)

George IV when Prince of Wales, by Sir William Beechey. (*Metropolitan Museum of Art*)

Thomas Orde-Powlett, 1st Baron Bolton.

Jean Mary Orde-Powlett, Lady Bolton, sketched by her husband. (*North Yorkshire County Records Office*)

George, Prince of Denmark, engraving after Sir Godfrey Kneller. (*Yale Center for British Art, Paul Mellon Collection*)

The popular Protestant heir was Sophia of Hanover, daughter of Bohemia's Winter King and Queen (and therefore granddaughter of James I and sister to (the deceased) Prince Rupert of the Rhine). Sophia was in her seventies by the time she was fixed in the succession to the British throne, but she was fit and healthy. More importantly, Sophia had a clutch of legitimately-born children

Miniature of John Churchill, 1st Duke of Marlborough by Christian Friedrich Zincke. (*Cleveland Museum of Art*)

Sarah Jennings, Duchess of Marlborough. (*Nationalmuseum, Sweden*)

and grandchildren to inherit. Despite rumours of plots and schemes, Sophia had no intention of usurping Anne and an uneasy reconciliation took place between the Duke of Bolton and the queen, and also with John Churchill, Duke of Marlborough.

Bolton's daughter Frances caused a minor scandal when she eloped with John, Viscount Mordaunt of Avalon, the 3rd Earl of Peterborough's eldest son. Two years earlier, Mordaunt had been rejected by the Duke of Marlborough as a suitor for the hand of his daughter Mary. Marlborough said of John, 'I have heard that he is what they call a rascal, which can never make a good husband.' Perhaps the Duke of Bolton had a similar view on the man his daughter fell in love with, causing the couple to elope. With no marriage settlement in place, Frances brought nothing to the marriage, a fact that wasn't lost on John's family, who disapproved of the match every bit as much as the Powletts. Mordaunt, a military man, had recently suffered such a devastating injury to his arm in battle that it had to be amputated. After hearing of his marriage to Lady Frances Powlett, Mordaunt's mother Carey, Countess of Peterborough, remarked with biting acidity that John, by his 'unhappy marriage had shown the deepest ingratitude: "O that Heaven had left him no hand to dispose of!"'[6]

The Duke of Queensberry presenting the Act of Union to Queen Anne. (*New York Public Library*)

As the years passed, the former differences between Bolton and his monarch were forgotten, the situation improved by the Marlboroughs' own fall from grace. In 1705, the same year in which Bolton's daughter Frances eloped with the Viscount Mordaunt, the duke entertained the queen and Prince George of Denmark at Hackwood. With this renewed royal favour, Bolton was able to gain a position as one of the commissioners who brought about the Act of Union. The Act, despite opposition from Scotland but with the wholehearted support of Queen Anne, whose lifelong wish it was, united the Parliaments of England and Scotland to form one Parliament of Great Britain. It also created Great Britain, uniting England, Wales and Scotland into one kingdom in an act of political union that came into effect on 1 May 1707. The Jacobite lord, John Erskine, Earl of Mar (known as 'Bobbing John' as he changed his loyalties between Whig, Tory, Jacobite and Hanoverian as it suited him) told the queen he doubted not 'but your subjects will always bless your Majesty for this amongst the other great things you have done, and that your memory will be famous and admired in all succeeding ages'. Despite Bobbing John's praise and the queen's own wish that 'the whole island [would now be] joined in affection', there wasn't much joy felt north of the Scottish border. The act – a 'bad bargain' – was unpopular with most of the Scots and did nothing to quell the rising tide of Jacobinism that posed such a threat to the continuance of a Protestant monarchy.

More rewards in the form of official positions came the way of the duke. In particular, he was granted the Wardenship of the New Forest. Near to Lyndhurst is a spot known as Bolton's Bench and legend says that the beautiful Henrietta, Duchess of Bolton made it something of a resort in the warmer months, sitting on a hillock and enjoying the idyllic scenery. A yew tree was planted on the spot, surrounded by a fixed bench, and it was named in memory of the duchess who first sat there.[7]

Chapter Nine

The Polly Peerage

'The famous Polly, Duchess of Bolton, is dead, having, after a life of merit, relapsed into her Pollyhood. Two years ago, ill at Tunbridge, she picked up an Irish surgeon. When she was dying, this fellow sent for a lawyer to make her will, but the man, finding who was to be her heir, instead of her children, refused to draw it. The Court of Chancery did furnish one other, not quite so scrupulous, and her three sons have but a thousand pounds apiece, the surgeon about nine thousand.'[1]

Charles, 8th Marquess of Winchester and future 3rd Duke of Bolton, had a tangled love life and the woman who captured his heart was, much to the despair of his family, the actress who was the first to make the role of Polly Peachum in *The Beggar's Opera* her own.

Even as a child, the signs were all too evident. In his grandfather's lifetime, the young lord was sent to the Palace School in Enfield for his education which was, by all accounts, an unmitigated disaster. The Palace School occupied an old Elizabethan manor house that had once belonged to Queen Elizabeth I and was a rival, fee-paying boarding school to the Enfield Grammar School. Dr Robert Uvedale was the headmaster of both establishments. Uvedale was accused of neglecting his grammar school pupils in favour of his boarders, but his energies were wasted on young Master Powlett. Complaining about his problematic pupil, Uvedale said that Wiltshire 'declines all business, and refuses to be governed, absenting himself from school, and by no persuasion will be prevayl'd upon to follow his studies, but takes what liberty hee thinks fitt upon all occasions.' The 14-year-old lad was, in fact, head over heels in love with a young girl, to the detriment of his studies. It would become a common theme throughout his life.[2]

Instead of continuing his studies at Enfield, Charles was sent abroad with an old friend of the family, Anthony Ashley Cooper, 3rd Earl of Shaftesbury (whose grandfather had been appointed as the 5th Marquess of Winchester's

Queen Elizabeth's Palace, Enfield (the 3rd Duke of Bolton's school) from *Antiquarian Repertory*, vol. 1, 1807.

children's guardian after the fall of Basing House at the hands of Cromwell's men). Charles remained on mainland Europe until August 1704, probably spending most time at Rotterdam in the Netherlands where Shaftesbury had settled. From the death in 1699 of his grandfather, Charles held the title of Marquess of Winchester, while his father became the 2nd Duke of Bolton. (Henceforth, until he becomes the 3rd Duke of Bolton, we will refer to the younger Charles as Winchester or simply as Charles, and his father as the duke or Bolton.) By February 1712, Charles was back in London and one of 'a parcel of drunken Whiggish lords' with too much time on their hands. As Jonathan Swift wrote to his friend Esther Johnson (who was perhaps Swift's secret wife), these lords descended on the chocolate houses to 'rail aloud at the

Tories, and have challenges sent them, and the next morning come and beg pardon. General Ross was like to swinge the Marquis of Winchester for this trick t'other day.'[3]

A year later, under instructions from his father to snare a wealthy bride, Lord Winchester's wandering eyes fell upon an innocent, well-brought-up heiress. Lady Anne Vaughan was the only child of the Earl of Carbery (of Golden Grove, Carmarthenshire), and she had inherited all her father's wealth and estates after he dropped dead of an apoplexy at his Chelsea home. The unorthodox, independent and well-travelled Lady Mary Wortley Montagu, Lady Anne's friend (and possibly also a distant relative), thought the young woman to be in 'the most perilous and pitiable incident to womankind; that of a great heiress at her own free disposal.' William Berkeley, 4th Baron Berkeley of Stratton watched the ensuing drama and noted that 'there is such running after my Lord Carbery's rich daughter as you never saw. My Lord Lumley makes the greatest bustle, but whether the most in favour, I do not know. My Lord Winchester and Lord Hertford are also in pursuit.' Lord Lumley was Richard, eldest surviving son and heir to the Earl of Scarborough (and, by a curious twist, he was later the 2nd Earl of Scarborough and the same man who committed suicide in the house subsequently occupied by the 5th Duke of Bolton). Algernon Seymour, Earl of Hertford and later the 7th Duke of Somerset, was fabulously rich, heir not only to his father's estates but also those of his mother (the sole heiress of her father, the 11th Earl of Northumberland). Lord Hertford would, with hindsight, have been the better catch for Lady Anne, who ought to have known better. Her own father was notorious for his licentious morals (he was the 'lewdest fellow of the age', according to Samuel Pepys), but Anne had been educated in almost total isolation by a devout governess and knew little of the world. Charles, Lord Winchester was handsome, smooth-tongued, titled and well-connected. The fact that he was also a libertine of the first order was overlooked by poor Anne, who shunned her other admirers and readily accepted Charles's hand in marriage. Lord Berkeley was one of the first to hear the news: 'My Lord Winchester is to be the happy man that marries my Lady Anne Vaughan. They say it is concluded.' Indeed it was, and the summer wedding took place at St James's in Piccadilly, Westminster.[4]

Once Charles had landed his virtuous heiress, he was no longer interested in anything other than her money and, according to Lady Mary Wortley Montagu, made his wife 'an early confession of his aversion' (popular opinion said that he was ungallant enough to drop this bombshell as the couple left the church). The newly-wed Marchioness of Winchester was informed by her

Thought to be a portrait of Lady Mary Wortley Montagu by Sir Godfrey Kneller. (*Yale Center for British Art, Paul Mellon Collection*)

husband that he never had been nor ever would be faithful to her. He was as good as his word, entertaining a string of lovers, and Lady Anne accepted the situation with sadness. (The marquess's rapacious sexual appetite (for everyone but his wife) might have been fired by the variety of cakes containing ambergris known to be made by his cook, John Nott. Although its main use was in perfume, ambergris was also considered an aphrodisiac. Madame de Pompadour, mistress of Louis XV of France, famously dined on chocolate flavoured with ambergris and vanilla.)[5] '[Lady Anne] thought it impossible not to find gratitude, though she failed to give passion; and upon this threw away her estate, was despised by her husband, and laughed at by the public.'[6]

Horace Walpole, who managed to have an opinion on the matter even though he was not even born at the time of the marriage, referred to the union in a letter to a friend, written many decades later. He believed that the marriage was, in fact, no true marriage at all, writing in a cruel jibe of Lady Anne to say that, 'unluckily she was a monster, so ugly, that [Winchester], being forced by his father to marry her for her great fortune, was believed never to have consummated [the match], and parted from her as soon as his father died.' For all Walpole's gossip, the portrait of Lady Anne, painted by Godfrey Kneller around the time of her marriage, does not show the woman he describes: 'Staring from the canvas, Anne looks intelligent and amiable if a little downcast and serious, and could anyone blame her for that?'[7]

The Marquess and Marchioness of Winchester lived separate lives following their unfortunate marriage, he resident in the hustle and bustle of London with its gentlemen's clubs, coffee houses and pleasure palaces, and she in the obscurity of their country estates, and there wasn't anything unusual in this in an age of arranged marriages among the aristocracy. However, with the need for a son and heir, both husband and wife were expected to do their duty; in this case, it appears that neither was inclined to intimacy with the other. The new marchioness was humiliated by her husband's aversion to her and his very public philandering.

Notwithstanding his treatment of his wife, public offices came thick and fast for Lord Winchester, including some due to his wife's Welsh influence (Charles became both MP for Carmarthen and Lord Lieutenant of the counties of Carmarthen and Glamorgan in 1715), but one position was more important than these: in the mid-1710s, Charles was appointed a Gentleman of the Bedchamber to George, Prince of Wales (later George II).

During the last year of Queen Anne's life, when her health gave concern and the matter of the succession was of the utmost importance, Parliament was divided between the Jacobite lords who favoured the Pretender and those who looked to Hanover and a Protestant monarch. There was also an ongoing controversy concerning the South Sea Company, particularly in connection with profits from the scheme that had been reserved for the queen and her financial advisor. Two of the biggest investors in the company were – individually – the Duke and Duchess of Marlborough; for a time, if they had the money to do so, women were able to play the London Stock Exchange (for aristocratic women, it was seen as another form of gambling). In the midst of all the uncertainty, in July 1714 the queen entered the house leaning upon the arm of the Duke of Bolton who was now in high favour. Much good it would do him, though; less than a month later, Anne was dead at 49 years of age, her body and health wrecked by multiple pregnancies and obesity.

Towards the end of Queen Anne's life, all eyes had turned to the next Protestant heir presumptive, Sophia, Electress of Hanover. Although Sophia was much older than her cousin, she was still in excellent health and there was no reason to suspect that she would not, for a short while and in her dotage, take the crown of England. Then events overtook the planned succession. Two months before Anne's demise, Sophia caused a shock when she dropped dead after running to shelter following a sudden summer downpour in her German palace, Herrenhausen. It was Sophia's eldest son, George, ruler of the Duchy and Electorate of Brunswick-Lüneburg in Hanover, who took the British throne in 1714, despite a few hiccups and teething problems. One huge stumbling block for the new king was his inability to speak the language of his subjects: decades earlier, Prince Rupert had wanted to fund a stay in England for his nephew so the boy could learn the people's ways and the language. Sophia had refused and now the language barrier proved a problem, but not an insurmountable one. The Duke of Bolton was one of the men instrumental in ensuring that the Hanoverian succession went without a hitch and luckily, both he and his new king were proficient in French, so that was the language in which they wrote and conversed.

King George I and his eldest son, also named George, arrived in London at the end of September to much pomp and ceremony. The younger George was invested as Prince of Wales and several peers' sons were appointed as his Gentlemen of the Bedchamber including Charles Powlett, Marquess of Winchester. The role was a coveted one as it brought the holder into direct and close contact with the monarchy: such Gentlemen provided companionship but also helped the prince to dress, waited on him at his table and guarded his bedchamber and water closet. Charles now had the friendship and ear of

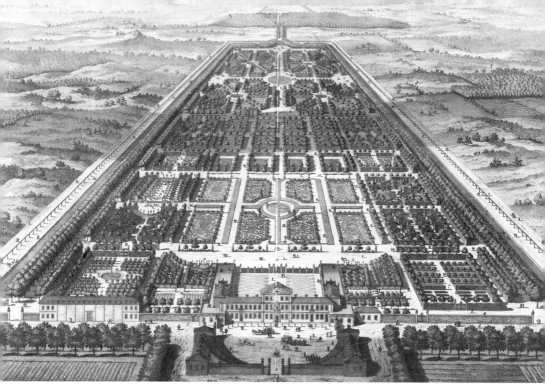

Herrenhausen Palace and Gardens. (*AxelHH/Wikimedia Commons/PD-US/CC-BY-SA-3.0*)

Sophia Charlotte, Electress of Hanover
(Prince Rupert's sister and mother
of George I) by Johan David Swartz.
(*Nationalmuseum, Sweden*)

George, Prince of Wales (later George II)
after Georg Wilhelm Lafontaine.
(*Rijksmuseum*)

the heir to the throne, a suitable reward for his father's efforts to stabilize the succession and new Hanoverian reign.[8]

George I was struck by the beauty of Henrietta, Duchess of Bolton, and her royal ancestry. She had never been given much prominence at Queen Anne's court, but now Henrietta was a frequent and welcome guest. She too received a position in the royal household when she was appointed one of the six Ladies of the Bedchamber (ladies-in-waiting) to Caroline of Ansbach, the new Princess of Wales. It was a well-regarded position, and one that could only be held by a peeress. While nominally there to provide companionship, it gave the women concerned a direct route to royal privilege and a modicum of power as they used feminine wiles to gently influence matters of state. (The Prince of Wales's mistress, Henrietta Howard, was also a Lady of the Bedchamber to the princess.)

In a public mark of her status at the new court, Henrietta was placed in a prominent position on one balmy summer evening in July 1717. In a

Nineteenth-century depiction of the royal barge on the Thames during the first performance of Handel's *Water Music*, by Edouard Jean Conrad Hamman. (*Sir Gawain/Wikimedia Commons/PD-US/CC-BY-SA-3.0*)

glittering display, the royal barge set off from Whitehall Palace to cruise up the Thames towards Chelsea. A second barge, containing around fifty musicians, accompanied them, playing what would be the first performance of the composer George Frideric Handel's *Water Music* suite, and a whole host of smaller boats and barges thronged alongside to enjoy the glitzy spectacle. In the royal barge, alongside King George I were six high-ranking lords and ladies who were the new king's particular favourites: the Duchess of Newcastle, the Duke of Kingston, the Earl of Orkney, the Countess of Godolphin, the king's German mistress Sophia Charlotte von Kielmansegg and, seated next to the king, Henrietta, Duchess of Bolton.

The Duke of Bolton was only in his mid-fifties but was suffering from ill health, so Henrietta would often appear without her husband at her side. It was almost five years later, in the first month of 1722, that the 2nd Duke of Bolton died of pleurisy in his home on Dover Street, London. As soon as his scapegrace son heard the news, he let it be known that he was, to all intents and purposes, separated from his hated wife. While divorce was possible, it would expose them to public censure and humiliation, and wasn't an option either of the couple wished to pursue. Besides, Charles was doing very well from his wife's connections and while he was more than happy to have nothing to do with her, he was loath to lose her family influence. Anne, now Duchess of Bolton whether her husband liked it or not, was well thought of and Charles – in a rare sensible moment – chose the path of least resistance. He petitioned the House of Lords in order that his wife could independently raise money on the land she had brought to their marriage (by law it was owned by Charles but, in the circumstances, he recognized Anne's moral right to it). It was a symbolic act which severed the majority of her ties to and claims upon her reprobate husband and allowed Anne to live in comfortable retirement. In 1726, Bolton (or the duke, as we will now refer to him) accepted the governorship of the Isle of Wight and, probably to his wife's relief, was not seen much in London for a couple of years. He was back, however, in time to witness the latest theatrical sensation.

On 29 January 1728, John Gay's *The Beggar's Opera* opened at the Lincoln's Inn Fields Theatre in London. It was an instant success and made stars of its performers, in particular a young actress named Lavinia Fenton who had been plucked from the London streets and placed on the stage. *The Beggar's Opera* turned her into a star overnight.

The opera was described as a Newgate pastoral, a satire depicting thieves and whores and poking fun at notorious criminals, politicians and personalities.

A Fleet Wedding, 1747. (*Yale University, Lewis Walpole Library*)

Lavinia took on the role of Polly Peachum, the daughter of Mr Peachum, a tavern landlord and leader of a gang of criminals; Polly falls in love with the anti-hero of the opera, Macheath, a highwayman. Her innocent and youthful beauty garnered Lavinia a veritable army of male admirers, chief among them Charles Powlett, 3rd Duke of Bolton who attended the theatre almost every night; so often, in fact, that when William Hogarth painted a scene from *The Beggar's Opera* depicting Lavinia as Polly on the stage, the duke was shown in a box to the right. Well and truly captivated, the duke cared nothing for Lavinia's low birth: it was said that she was illegitimate, her father a naval lieutenant named Beswick who sailed before she was born, leaving behind nothing but an empty promise to return and wed her mother. When he failed to do so, 'Mrs Beswick' married a Mr Fenton instead, a coffee house keeper from Charing Cross. The truth is a little more prosaic: during May 1710 in a clandestine wedding at the Fleet Prison (which was used for these ceremonies as it was believed to be outside the jurisdiction of the church), Peter Beswick,

Charing Cross, with the Statue of King Charles I by Joseph Nickolls, c.1750. (*Yale Center for British Art, Paul Mellon Collection*)

a victualler, married Elizabeth Neal. Both parties were from Wapping in the East End of London and their daughter, Lavinia, was born almost exactly five months later and christened at St Margaret's in Westminster. Legend says that, as a young adolescent, Lavinia tried out the roles of whore, waitress and barmaid before taking to the stage, but once in the spotlight she proved to be a natural actress, clever and witty with a vivacious personality.[9]

The estrangement between the Duke and Duchess of Bolton was now permanent and, as Anne was provided for (she had been granted £1,000 a year from the profits of her estates to spend as she wished), the duke was ready to begin a new chapter of his life. Lavinia appeared in his orbit at the perfect time and for her, Bolton was prepared to overlook everything else. Miss Fenton appeared on the stage as Polly Peachum some sixty-two times, and the duke sat in the box on the side of the stage for many of those performances, gazing with adoration at the young actress. Except, perhaps, for the one night when, in what may have been a cruel joke or even an act of defiance on the part of the duchess, Bolton took his seat in company with his long-suffering wife. Lavinia wasn't short of admirers and needed a bodyguard to keep them at bay as she left the theatre each night, but the smitten duke took precedence. He also offered her a guaranteed income: £400 a year and £200 even if he lost interest in her. Lavinia acquiesced, and the duke took her off the stage and into his keeping, heedless as to what his friends and family would say. He provided a fine London townhouse for Lavinia at No. 6 Cork Street in Mayfair, a small and pleasant thoroughfare set on the edge of the new development and within view of open countryside, although it would soon be swallowed up in the urban

Detail from *The Beggar's Opera* by William Hogarth, showing Lavinia kneeling on the stage and the 3rd Duke of Bolton seated at the far right, watching her. (*Yale Center for British Art, Paul Mellon Collection*)

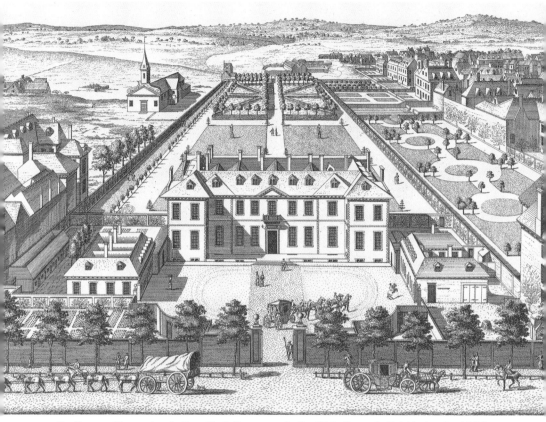

Burlington House, just before Cork Street was built. (*Yale Center for British Art, Paul Mellon Collection*)

sprawl; a few steps to the end of the street would bring Lavinia to the gardens of the palatial Burlington House on Piccadilly. Her next-door neighbour was the Welsh MP Erasmus Lewis, a great friend of the author Jonathan Swift and the poet Alexander Pope. At No. 2 was Dr Arbuthnot who, at the time, was guardian of Peter the Wild Boy and overseeing his education. Peter had been found about three years earlier, living feral in a wooded area near Hanover in Germany and brought to England where he was presented to the king and queen as a curiosity. Despite Dr Arbuthnot's best endeavours, Peter never did learn how to read or write.[10]

After many years of whoring, Bolton settled down into a happy domestic intimacy. The one fly in the ointment was, of course, that he was still married to Lady Anne and whatever Lavinia's charms, he still didn't press for a divorce.

While he could – and did – have sons with Lavinia, none could inherit either the dukedom or his estates.

Lavinia had no wish to be buried in obscurity at Bolton Hall among the wilds of the North Yorkshire moors. Instead, she left Cork Street to play mistress of

Lavinia Fenton, engraving after John Ellys. (*Yale University, Lewis Walpole Library*)

Westcombe Manor, Greenwich, 1779. (*Yale Center for British Art, Paul Mellon Collection*)

the house at Hackwood, but – perhaps facing opposition from his family at Lavinia's presence there – the duke soon took the lease on Westcombe House, a mansion in Greenwich. There he housed his new family, which quickly grew. Lavinia fell pregnant almost straight away and a son, Charles, was born just after Christmas Day. Wasting no time at all, a second son, Percy was born less than two years later and then there was a gap of several years until the birth of their third son, Horatio Armand. This youngest son's unusual middle name could denote that his cousin, Charles Armand Powlett (son of Lord William) stood as the boy's godfather.[11]

Westcombe House was an elegant, new-built mansion, standing in an idyllic location almost opposite the entrance to Greenwich Park. The prospect from the terrace near the house was beautiful, commanding the windings of the Thames with Shooter's Hill and the intervening woodland. Lavinia had come

Two Hunters belonging to his Grace, the Duke of Bolton, 1738. (*Yale Center for British Art, Paul Mellon Collection*)

a long way from her modest childhood in a cramped Charing Cross coffee house.[12]

The small albeit unconventional family lived happily, Lavinia in busy domesticity and Bolton pursuing the dual lifestyles of family man and nobleman. He devoted much time to the Bolton stud; equine pursuits were engrained in the Powlett dynasty's blood and the duke carried on his family's tradition, breeding and racing several noted thoroughbreds and hunters. To make life easier, in 1728 the duke took a lease on a Newmarket mansion, situated in an ideal position to enjoy the races. The duke and Lavinia also travelled extensively around mainland Europe where Lavinia's past life as an actress could be more easily overlooked. During their journeys, they purchased several fine works of art including at least four portraits by the Italian painter Giovanni Antonio Canal (better known as Canaletto), bought (for 100 gold Venetian coins, known as zecchini, for the set) from the artist in the late 1730s during one of their frequent visits to Venice.[13]

Chapter Ten

His Brother's Heir

The 2nd Duke of Bolton's second son Henry (known as Harry), was the 'spare heir' and an army officer who served in Portugal as aide-de-camp to the French Huguenot Earl of Galway, Henri de Massue and then as captain of a troop of dragoons at the siege of Preston in 1715 during the first Jacobite uprising. (After his brother had become the 3rd Duke of Bolton, Harry, as his brother's heir, was ineligible to bear the family's lesser title of Marquess of Winchester, which could only be given to the eldest (legitimate) son of a duke and so was known as Lord Harry Powlett during his brother's lifetime.)

Harry married Catherine Parry (the daughter of Francis Parry of Oakfield (formerly Wokefield) in Berkshire, a gentleman who had been envoy to Portugal during the reign of Charles II) and had four children, two sons who were named – in the Powletts' continued confusing and unimaginative manner – exactly as in the previous generation, Charles and Harry, and two daughters. He also had an illegitimate son by an unknown lady – probably a Miss Perry as that was the surname used by the boy, although it is perplexingly similar to his wife's surname – and to confound things further, this son shared the first name of Lord Harry's eldest legitimate child, Charles. Charles Perry was born before his father's marriage to Catherine Parry, hence the re-use of the name when the heir to the title was born, but the boys seem to have been brought up together. They were very close as adults, suggesting an intimacy formed in childhood.

Catherine had married Lord Harry Powlett by 1716 when their daughter Henrietta was born (named in honour of the 2nd duke's last wife Henrietta Crofts who was still living); Charles, the eldest son, was born on 22 February 1718 followed by a brother, Harry, two years later and lastly another daughter, named Catherine for her mother. With the family estates all in the possession of the 3rd Duke of Bolton, Lord Harry was given the use of one of the lesser manors. His family made their home at Edington in Wiltshire in a large, late-medieval house known as the Priory House which had once been a religious building.[1]

The remains of the Priory House at Edington, Wiltshire from the *Gentleman's Magazine*, vol. 26, September 1846.

Edington has a long history: in 878 King Alfred defeated the Viking army at the Battle of Edington and he later granted the manor to his wife, Ealhswith. In the Middle Ages, a priory dedicated to the Augustinian order of the Brothers of Penitence (or the *Bonshommes*), an Augustinian order, was founded and, as it was on the route taken by pilgrims travelling between Bath and Salisbury, it prospered until the dissolution of the monasteries in 1539 when, during the conflict between Henry VIII and the Catholic Church, the king oversaw the closure of many religious institutions while he appropriated their assets, benefitting himself and his allies. Edington was one of these and was granted to William Powlett, 1st Marquess of Winchester in 1550 during the reign of Edward VI.[2]

Under the ownership of the Powletts, Edington Priory became a manor house, although all that now remains of the original monastic buildings are a few doorways and a buttress. Largely remodelled in the 1600s, by the time Lord Harry moved in, the manor house was, in the eighteenth century, considered an old-fashioned, dark and somewhat ugly building, incomparable to the Italianate and neoclassical-influenced country mansions being built by other aristocratic families. Lord Harry's situation was one of comfortable gentility rather than aristocratic affluence though, and he lived more as a country squire. Lord Harry Powlett's two sons Charles and Harry were both educated at Winchester College as fee-paying commoners between 1728 and 1729; Charles Perry was educated elsewhere. The headmaster of the college at that time was John Burton, who took into his chambers a specially-selected number of boys from noble families rather than letting them take lodgings in the town of Winchester itself, and the Powlett boys were two of these.

While his younger brother left to enter the new naval academy at Portsmouth Dockyard, destined for a career on the high seas (thanks to his family's influence, the Honourable Harry Powlett junior was captain of a naval ship by the time he was 20 years of age), Charles went up to Cambridge to take his degree. A military career initially seemed to beckon for Charles, and in 1737 he joined the 1st Foot Guards (now known as the Grenadier Guards) as an ensign. It was a fitting regiment for him given his family background; the 1st Foot Guards' origins were as Charles II's bodyguard during his last decade in exile before the restoration of the monarchy. It was a period of relative peace when Charles enlisted, and perhaps the young Charles found life in a barracks insufferably dull, for he soon sold his commission. Instead, he became a lieutenant colonel in the Hampshire militia and stood as both MP and mayor for Lymington, a port and market town situated between the New Forest and the Solent. Lymington had long been held by a member of the family; Charles's great-uncle William Powlett (the 1st Duke of Bolton's second son) and his uncle Nassau Powlett (son of the 2nd Duke of Bolton and Henrietta Crofts) had both been one of the town's two MPs. That is not to say, though, that Colonel Charles Powlett stood for the seat with the approbation of his uncle, the 3rd Duke of Bolton. In fact, it was completely the opposite. To defeat the 3rd duke, who was scheming to obtain sole control of the borough of Lymington, Charles and the town's other MP, Harry Burrard worked together to thwart his aims. They called a hasty meeting, created new freemen and secured their majority; it was an alliance that the livid duke described as 'the greatest treachery'. Once elected, Charles used his name and influence in the county but was content to take a back seat in his political partnership with Burrard, who said that once the two had

> established our interest, which we kept up in mutual harmony, without again adding to the number of our burgesses, during Colonel Charles Powlett's life. Nothing transpired in any matter relative to the borough till we had agreed between ourselves on the point. He left the management of everything to me, and never suffered anybody else to interfere with the business of the borough.[3]

The Royal Dockyard at Portsmouth, 1790 by Robert Dodd. (*Yale Center for British Art, Paul Mellon Collection*)

The summer of 1751 saw the arrival of the Duke of Bolton and Lavinia at Aix-en-Provence in southern France, the duke travelling in the hope of a recovery because, for some time, he had suffered from a weakness in his legs and feet: 'I have bien [*sic*] told that a Warmer Climate and a Clearer Air such as the South of France, wou'd give me better health than I have had for some years.'[4]

Travelling with them was the duke's protégé, the Reverend Joseph Warton, a Hampshire cleric. Nominally there purely to accompany the duke and provide some much-needed male company for Bolton (and in spite of Warton's religious distaste of the couple's living arrangements), in reality Warton was there for an entirely different but much more important reason. Back in London, the Duchess of Bolton had also been unwell for several months and the duke was on tenterhooks merely waiting for news of her death to reach him before marrying Lavinia. Joseph Warton was with the duke and Lavinia so he could perform the ceremony without delay. The poor duchess, lingering in a painful illness at her London townhouse in Upper Grosvenor Street during a dreary wet summer, knew that her passing would be met with celebrations by

Bolton and her 'husband's whore'. She died at the end of September, clinging to life just long enough to thwart her husband's plans by a few days, at least. Warton had been called home just before the news reached Aix-en-Provence and so a messenger was despatched to the king's envoy at Turin, William Henry Nassau de Zuylestein, 4th Earl of Rochford. The earl, as a Protestant envoy in a Catholic country, was allowed to maintain a chapel within his house for the use of his family and countrymen. Rochford and he sent his chaplain, a London-born Oxford graduate of Huguenot descent named Lewis de Visme, to the duke at Aix-en-Provence. The wedding ceremony took place just a month after Lady Anne's death on 21 October 1751, with no regard for the normal convention of a period of mourning.[5] 'They write from Aix in Provence, that his Grace the Duke of Bolton was lately married there, to Mrs Fenton; who formerly gave the Town great pleasure in a publick character.'

Lavinia Fenton, after twenty-three years of waiting, was the new Duchess of Bolton and de Visme was well-rewarded for his service. A combination of the warm weather and news from England worked wonders on Bolton's health; the newly-wed duke and duchess honeymooned on the continent over the winter and discreetly returned to England the following spring when the initial gossip over their marriage had died down. Once back in the country, the duke presented de Visme to the lucrative living of Bigbury-on-Sea in Devon, and the couple retired to Hackwood. There the gentry of Basingstoke, and the Corporation and mayor, visited the Duke and Duchess of Bolton at Hackwood, and the next day at Basingstoke 'his Grace gave them a grand Entertainment ... the bells continued ringing the whole day, and nothing but mirth and jollity went forward, and joy appear'd in every one's countenance.' It was almost everything Lavinia could have hoped for, and there was perhaps even more cause for celebration. A single newspaper report survives to hint at an event that may have changed the whole course of the Bolton dynasty. Lavinia, at the age of 42, had fallen pregnant not long after her wedding. 'Her Grace the Dutchess of Bolton, who is far advanced in her Pregnancy, is coming to Town from his Grace's Seat at Hackwood, in order to lye-in.' If this report was true, and Lavinia was to be delivered of a son, at last the duke would have the heir he had longed for. It wasn't to be; if Lavinia was indeed pregnant, the child didn't survive.[6]

Life settled back into a routine, but for all too short a time as the duke was plagued by ill health. When the noted bluestocking Elizabeth Montagu saw him at Bath during the summer of 1753, she didn't think he would last out the month. The dry summer and miraculous Bath waters worked their wonders

Hackwood Park, 1775, engraving after Paul Sandby. (*British Library*)

though, and when she next saw him, Elizabeth was 'amazed at the amendment'. It was a short respite, however, and the following year the duke had relapsed. Together with Lavinia, Bolton was at Tunbridge Wells, hoping that drinking the iron-rich waters of the town's Chalybeate Spring would perfect a cure. It was during his visit that the 3rd Duke of Bolton died on 26 August 1754, the waters having failed to take any effect. With no legitimate heirs, while he could leave his personal wealth and possessions to Lavinia and their three sons, the estates and ducal title were inherited by his younger brother, Harry Powlett.[7]

Bolton and Lavinia's sons grew up to join the clergy, the navy and the army respectively. (Horatio Armand, at the age of 16, was apprenticed to a City of London merchant but decided that a military life was preferable to one of business, and Charles, the eldest, tried out the army before settling on the

Lady Elizabeth Montagu, 1756, engraving after Sir Joshua Reynolds. (*Yale Center for British Art, Paul Mellon Collection*)

church.) Lavinia, in her widowhood, turned to the man who had married her to the duke and appointed Lewis de Visme as her personal chaplain. As the gossip, Horace Walpole put it, Lavinia, now the Dowager Duchess of Bolton, 'after a life of merit relapsed into her Pollyhood'. She became entangled with George Kelley, a Tunbridge Wells surgeon and, to the disgust of her sons, named him as her executor and residuary legatee in her will. Lavinia retained Westcombe House for the remainder of her life, and it was there she died, on a cold January day in 1760. She was buried 10 days later at St Alfege's Church in Greenwich and Westcombe House passed to her eldest son. In a letter to

Although Mary was gentry rather than aristocracy, there was no reason why she would not be considered a suitable bride for the heir to a dukedom. True, she had no fortune, but if this had been of prime importance to Lord Winchester, then he would have put her aside and married an heiress (just as his contemporary, Sackville Tufton, 8th Earl of Thanet did in 1767 when he turned his mistress, the courtesan Nelly O'Brien (mother of his two sons and pregnant with a third) out of the home they had shared, in preparation for his marriage to the wealthy daughter of Lord John Sackville). Mary Banks Brown's shady past might have been a concern in the eyes of the wider family (and his father's approbation was important), but Lavinia Fenton still remained the Dowager Duchess of Bolton and the men of the family had long had a reputation for eccentricity, so eyebrows wouldn't have been raised too much. No, it was something else that prohibited a lawful union and that was most probably an earlier marriage contracted by Mary, hinted at by the inclusion of Brown in her name.[13]

The 'polite' description of Mary as Winchester's housekeeper has a contemporary echo in the life of Kitty Fisher, a well-known mid-eighteenth-century courtesan who inspired the following nursery rhyme:

> Lucy Locket lost her pocket,
> Kitty Fisher found it:
> The deuce a farthing was there in't –
> Only the binding round it.

Kitty was, for an all-too-brief period, the number one celebrity of her day until she 'retired' to the country with her lover; there, in the early 1760s, she lived in relative obscurity as his mistress, but for the sake of decency was named as his housekeeper and used an assumed name … just like Mary, she was known as Mrs Brown.[14]

Discretion in the matter of Winchester's private life was of the utmost concern; he had been one of the Grooms of the Bedchamber to Frederick, Prince of Wales from 1749 until 1751. That appointment ended with the prince's early death. For many years, the prince had presided over a rival court and he and the king had been at loggerheads, although they later reached a form of reconciliation. As a Groom of the Bedchamber, Winchester had attended to the prince in his more private moments, helping him dress and assisting him at his dining table. It was a coveted position: Winchester, who had then been known as Colonel Powlett, no doubt had one eye on the

Kitty Fisher, engraving after Sir Joshua Reynolds, 1759. (*Yale Center for British Art, Paul Mellon Collection*)

future and took a gamble in aligning himself with the prince rather than with the king. Had the prince lived to take the throne, it is a gamble that would have paid off but, even so, the position had brought with it a much-needed income of 400*l*. a year.[15]

We can be certain that Charles Powlett and Mary had been together as a couple since the latter months of 1750, if not before, as their daughter Jean Mary was born in the summer of 1751. She was christened in the grand

St Marylebone Church by James Miller, c.1773. (*Yale Center for British Art, Paul Mellon Collection*)

surroundings of St James's, Westminster as the daughter of Charles Powlett and Mary Banks Brown. There was no attempt to disguise her illegitimacy.

A further child, a son, was born almost five years later. Once again, at his christening (which took place in St Marylebone Church), the fact that his parents were not married was laid clear; his mother was named as Mrs Mary Banks Brown, while his father was recorded as 'Charles, Marquis of Winchester'. This son, whose name was Charles, had a short life; he had died before his father wrote his will in 1763 for there was no mention of him within. Why had Winchester not married Mary and given that son, had he lived, the opportunity to stand in line to inherit the Bolton dukedom? Despite their relationship having every sign of being a love-match, with the sensibilities of the era it is possible to think that Winchester, while he was still just the Honourable Colonel Powlett, had been keeping the door open for a marriage to a woman who would bring him riches and all the right connections. After his uncle's death, Winchester knew that – barring his own early demise – he would, in time, become Duke of Bolton, as would a son born to him. Whatever the prudence of marrying money, he was now able to pretty much suit himself in his private life and this all begs the question: with Mary pregnant again, why did Winchester not make her his marchioness?[16]

While it might not have been the conventional route, it would not have been out of the ordinary for a man to make a hasty marriage to his mistress to legitimize any children to be born. In fact, Winchester had an example very close to home which he could easily have followed. Charles Mordaunt, 4th Earl of Peterborough, was Winchester's cousin (Mordaunt's parents were Lady Frances Powlett, the 2nd Duke of Bolton's daughter, and John, Viscount Mordaunt). The earl abandoned his wife and two daughters for his lover who, coincidentally, also had the surname Brown: she was Robinaiana Brown from an impoverished but once noble family hailing from the Scottish borders. Robinaiana and Peterborough had several children, sons and a daughter, but as they were born out of wedlock none of those sons could inherit their father's peerage. Then the Countess of Peterborough died and Robinaiana was pregnant once more. Throwing any regard for a decent mourning period out the window, Peterborough hurried his mistress up the aisle, hoping the child she was carrying was a boy. The babe proved to be a girl, but within a year or two the new Countess of Peterborough gave birth to the long-awaited son. Despite having several older brothers, this youngest son's legitimacy of birth meant that he took precedence over them and was his father's heir. The Earl of Peterborough's marriage to Robinaiana Brown took place in early December 1755, when Mary Banks Brown would have been heavily pregnant. Winchester was a loving and devoted father and a husband to Mary in everything but name, but something prevented the couple from marrying. If it was a previous marriage, while a divorce was possible, it was by no means easy or guaranteed. The process would leave Mary open to gossip and ridicule and, at the end of it, the matter had to be put before the House of Lords who would have the final say. Winchester's peers would be voting, an excruciating embarrassment for him, and they could just have easily passed a bill that only granted a separation from 'bed and board', leaving Mary still legally married, as passing one that gave her the freedom to wed again. If indeed Mary was married, then she and Winchester's one hope would be the death of the man to whom she was wed. In the meantime, even after Charles had inherited the title and estates, Mary remained Mrs Brown. To the world at large she was the duke's housekeeper, but in actuality, albeit in private, she was mistress of his heart and home. Never, though, his wife.

Also what of Charles Perry, the 4th Duke of Bolton's eldest son, born out of wedlock and so ineligible to inherit the family title and estates? Perry joined the army and – with the help of his father – bought a commission as a lieutenant colonel and captain of a company in the Coldstream Foot Guards. He remained a resolute bachelor, known as an almighty gamester, betting – and winning – enormous sums of money. He ran with a somewhat disreputable crowd; Horace Walpole, the noted wit George James (Gilly) Williams and the eccentric George Selwyn referred to the colonel as 'our Perry'.

In the last few days of 1755, Colonel Perry was given command of the 57th Regiment of Foot. Eighteen months later, after a spell doing garrison duty in Ireland and renumbered as the 55th, Perry's regiment was sent to Nova Scotia to shore up the British troops stationed there during the Seven Years' War. (They were supposed to take part in an attack on the Fortress of Louisbourg, but this plan had been abandoned when the regiment reached Canada.) The 55th landed at the beginning of July 1757, and a short time later, at Halifax, Colonel Perry was dead. Although the newspapers tried to wallpaper over the cracks, calling the death 'sudden' and hinting at the colonel's 'weak constitution' and referring to Halifax's notorious coastal fogs, the truth of the matter was soon common gossip among London society. Colonel Perry was dead by his own hand; he had committed suicide by shooting himself. As Horace Walpole noted in a letter to Sir Horace Mann, the use of the word '*suddenly*' in connection with the reporting of a death 'is always at first construed to mean, *by a pistol*'. If the reason behind Colonel Perry's act was ever known, it was buried by the family. Perry had been fond of his half-brothers and cousins and they of him, and while the 3rd Duke of Bolton lived, they had all been on a more or less equal footing, despite the illegitimacy of Perry and the 3rd duke's three sons. Now, however, Perry's younger brothers took precedence over him. He wasn't even allowed to use the family surname. For a proud man, despite his military successes and aristocratic lifestyle, and regardless of private recognition by his family, the elevation of his younger siblings at his own expense must have come with a level of humiliation and perhaps a growing sense of despondency – especially to a noted gambler – at the hand that fate had dealt him in the lottery of birth.[17]

Before setting sail, Perry had written his will, adding one codicil. His brother Charles, Marquess of Winchester was named as the sole executor and received the residue of Perry's fortune and effects after the few bequests had been executed. Those bequests reveal the enormity of Perry's bank balance and suggest that he had indeed been a successful gamester. Lord Harry Powlett got 6,000*l.* and the three sons of the 3rd duke and Lavinia – Charles, Percy and Horatio Armand Powlett – received 5,000*l.* apiece.[18]

Harry Powlett's tenure as Duke of Bolton was of short duration; he died on 9 October 1759. His young grandsons were also both dead, although his granddaughter Mary Henrietta was a thriving 6-year-old. She would be the one surviving child from Harry junior's marriage to Mary Nunn, and Mary herself died in 1764.[19]

Chapter Eleven

The Duke and his Housekeeper

The wife of the 1st Duke of Bolton, whose inheritance provided the name of the peerage, was the daughter of a servant as well as the daughter of an earl, and Lavinia, Duchess of Bolton came from the slums of London. Mary Banks Brown, although well-born into an influential Lincolnshire family, never gained the title of duchess. She remained a mistress – a high-class courtesan – despite walking up the aisle of the May Fair Chapel for that one doomed attempt at a marriage to the man she loved.

Mary Banks was born at Bawtry, a small market town and inland river port on the border between Nottinghamshire and Yorkshire, not far away from Doncaster. The Great North Road (now known mundanely as the A638) which linked London to Edinburgh via the ancient city of York ran through Bawtry, so for most of the eighteenth century, the town buzzed with activity. Mary's father Robert Banks was local gentry from a good family; an attorney, he mixed in the upper echelons of provincial society and married twice. By his first wife Jane Wharton, he had a son, also named Robert. After Jane's death, Robert married again at Owston Ferry in Lincolnshire's Isle of Axholme to a woman named Ann Horsley. Five children followed in quick succession – John Horsley, Mary, Barnabas, Francis and Joseph – all born within the first eight years of the Banks' marriage.[1]

Mary's grandfather was the Reverend Robert Banks, but it was his younger brother Joseph who was to have all the success, and it is his descendants who are remembered today; Joseph Banks made a fortune buying and selling property, including estates that had been forfeit in the 1715 Jacobite rebellion. He was also one of the few who managed to make a profit before the South Sea bubble burst in 1720, when the price of the South Sea Company's stock rose above its true value and many fortunes were irredeemably lost. With his wealth, he bought Revesby Abbey in Lincolnshire which became the seat of his namesake son and descended through this branch of the family to the famed botanist Sir Joseph Banks (the first Joseph's great-grandson). Mary's father, meanwhile,

Engraving of Revesby Abbey, around 1805. (*Authors' own collection*)

was a provincial attorney with a numerous family and a propensity to live beyond his means as, within the first ten years of Mary's life, Robert Banks found himself indebted to his wealthy cousin:

> 17 March 1733.
> There is nothing but the necessity of my affairs could oblige me to give you this trouble, but as my estate is already in your hands, I cannot by any means raise moneys that I must pay in Town, or be ruined, but by your assistance… [I] hope you will prevent the ruin and destruction that may fall upon a family only for want of a seasonable relief …[2]

Perhaps it was a lifetime of depending upon the charity of relations that propelled Mary, the family's sole daughter, into the life of a kept mistress; a beauty and quick-witted too, what she lacked was a fortune. Faced with a crossroads in her life, Mary knew that she could either settle for a good marriage in the quiet backwater surroundings of her Bawtry home, or she could fling caution to the wind and live the high life on the arm of a gentleman of fortune. Somehow Mary spirited herself into the orbit of the handsome, gregarious but dissolute Zachary Harnage More who had come into a substantial fortune early in life and, with the help of his friends, was doing his best to run through it in double-quick time. (Zachary's wealth came from the alum mines on his north Yorkshire estate.) The fast-living crowd he ran with included Charles Powlett and probably Powlett's half-brother Charles Perry too. Nothing remains to say how Mary caught his eye (it might have been that Mary's brother Francis was also one of Zachary's band of merry men), but we can rest assured that any caution was well and truly flung into a prevailing gale when Mary dived headfirst into Zachary's world, and what a world it was! There were the usual gentlemanly vices – gambling, drinking and riotous hard living – but Zachary was involved in activities that ran even deeper into the sphere of dissolute abandonment. He was a member of the Club of Demoniacs who gathered at the twelfth-century Skelton Castle (aka Crazy Castle and the home of the writer, John Hall-Stevenson) near the stunning north Yorkshire coastline. Not quite at the level of Francis Dashwood's Hellfire Club, the men who gathered at Crazy Castle were a hard-drinking bunch with a love of erotica, licentious verse and fictitious alter egos. Other members of the Demoniacs included the writer Laurence Sterne; the actor and theatre manager David Garrick was an occasional guest. It does not take much of a stretch of the imagination to think that Charles Powlett was also present at the Crazy Castle revels, and that through his friendship with Zachary Harnage More he came to meet – and fall in love with – the beautiful Mary Banks.

When Charles Powlett met her, Mary was already a mother. She had, sometime around 1740 when she was 16 years of age, given birth to Zachary's daughter who she named Mary Charlotte Thornhill More. With Zachary forced to sell his estates to settle his vast array of debts, he could no longer take care of Mary and their daughter. Into the breach stepped the gallant Colonel Powlett. While Zachary's friends all chipped in to buy the ruined rake an ensign's commission in the army, Powlett provided an altogether different form of practical support, and took Mary and her young daughter into his Wiltshire home.[3]

The one member of Mary's family who stayed close to her throughout these years was her younger brother Francis. He had joined the navy and by 1759 was in command of the *Swallow* sloop of war. His prize money from the ships he captured and – after the death of Harry Powlett – his status as the new Duke of Bolton's pseudo brother-in-law gained him an entry to the *haut ton*. Captain Francis Banks also managed to capture the heart of a wealthy heiress, Christian, daughter of the Reverend Richard Green of Findon in Sussex; in 1760 the couple were married at St Luke's in Chelsea. It was to be a short marriage. Not

Lady with a fan,
c.1760 by Paul Sandby
(showing the fashion
of the era). (*Yale Center
for British Art, Paul
Mellon Collection*)

Chelsea in the mid-1700s. (*Yale Center for British Art, Paul Mellon Collection*)

long after the nuptials, Christian Banks wrote her will and left her fortune and estates in Essex to her husband, who she also named as her executor. She died from a violent fever while Francis was at sea, having only been a wife for six months.[4]

Upon ascending to the dukedom, Bolton had taken the lease on 32 Grosvenor Square and as soon as he, Mary and their two daughters (for Mary Charlotte was brought up as one of the family) moved in, he began a complete overhaul of the property. No expense was spared, and the noted architect James Vardy was employed to design everything from the casing on the front of the building, which gave it a plain mid-Georgian brick frontage, to the wall brackets that held the candles illuminating the house and everything in between. Mary Banks, bearing a confused jumble of names and referred to by the house's servants simply as Mrs Brown, might not have been invited to society events, but in her own London townhouse, decorated and furnished in the latest fashion, she could reign supreme as its mistress. She also presided at the country estates owned by the duke: Bolton Hall in North Yorkshire and Hackwood in Hampshire. When Vardy was finished at Grosvenor Square, the duke was so delighted with his work that he invited him to continue with the updates at Hackwood.[5]

Augusta, Princess of Wales, 1751, after Thomas Hudson. (*Yale Center for British Art, Paul Mellon Collection*)

John Stuart, 3rd
Earl of Bute. (*New
York Public Library*)

Political matters occupied Bolton in the early days of his dukedom. John Stuart, 3rd Earl of Bute, had, like Bolton, been one of Frederick, Prince of Wales's attendants before the prince's death. (Bute had been a Gentleman of the Bedchamber.) While he lived, the Prince of Wales's London residence, Leicester House (in Leicester Square), had become the headquarters of political opposition to the king's faction. Afterwards Bute, a Scot, had stayed in favour with the prince's widow Princess Augusta, and had been appointed as a tutor and advisor to her eldest son, Prince George. This left Bute well placed to influence the politics of and be at the heart of the next royal court. It also led to a huge degree of distrust from his peers, especially with the machinations of the political world in the last days of George II's pro-Hanoverian reign. Those who aligned themselves with Bute and the young George, Prince of Wales became known as the Leicester House interest.

This ill-feeling spilled over into the Hampshire by-election of 1759, which Bute attempted to influence. The seat, which had been held by Bolton while he was the Marquess of Winchester, had become vacant with his elevation to the dukedom. James Brydges, Marquess of Carnarvon (MP for Winchester), backed Sir Simeon Stuart, 3rd Baronet of Hartley Mauditt (a Hampshire gentleman) for the seat on the Leicester House interest, angering Bolton whose family had pretty much controlled Hampshire elections for decades. It was a Powlett seat and, if not held by a member of the family, would go to a man of their own choosing. What was supposed to be a gentlemanly debate after which the Hampshire gentry would obediently fall into line behind the Powletts' man (Henry Bilson Legge) and do away with the need for an expensive electoral battle descended into open anarchy. According to Brydges, Bolton's speech proposing Legge was 'much ridiculed' (Brydges, of course, thought his own speech 'very handsome' and noted it 'gained great applause'). After a majority of the Hampshire gentlemen present at the meeting threw their support behind Stuart, Bolton stormed out of the building. Even though Stuart stepped down from the contest three weeks later, tensions still simmered and – during the following year – spilled out into a challenge. Bolton had clearly inherited all the hot-headedness of his great-grandfather, the first duke. On an April morning, Bolton and Sir Simeon Stuart and their seconds met to settle their differences at Marylebone Fields' duelling ground.[6]

The two men fought with swords and Bolton looked set to win the contest, having sliced open Stuart's sword arm before the contest ended in ignominy when Bolton, trying to press home his advantage, slipped and dislocated his knee. Sir Simeon Stuart told Bolton to stand up, and when the duke refused, ordered him to plead for his life. Bolton, in agony from his fall and far too proud to do any such thing, called Stuart's bluff and refused. This left Stuart in something of a predicament until, with more common sense than had been displayed thus far, it was decided that, as both parties were injured, honour was satisfied and the quarrel was at an end.[7]

Later that year, on 25 October 1760, George II died and his 22-year-old grandson became George III. Alongside preparations for his coronation, the hunt began for a suitable wife for the new king. The choice soon fell upon Princess Charlotte of Mecklenburg-Strelitz and, with negotiations concluded, she travelled to England to meet and marry her new husband. The wedding took place in the early autumn of 1761 at the Chapel Royal in St James's Palace and then, two weeks later, the king and queen were crowned at Westminster Abbey. Despite the fact that he had aligned himself with opposing factions politically, Bolton played a key role in the day's ceremony: making one of the processions of peers of the realm, he carried the queen's crown.[8]

With the new king came a new ministry, one headed by the Earl of Bute who was prime minister for a short but turbulent time. Inflamed with tensions due to Britain's involvement in the Seven Years' War and hindered by political differences (Bute was a Tory but his ministry mostly Whig), the new prime minister was too close to the crown for comfort. The situation was viewed by the Whigs almost as a return to the kind of absolute monarchy not witnessed in the country since the time of Charles I. Several peers were sacked from their offices (William Cavendish, 4th Duke of Devonshire and Lord Chancellor under the former administration, refused to attend a Cabinet meeting and so the king summarily dismissed him from his position). While the 3rd and 4th Dukes of Bolton had remained reasonably neutral in the political sphere, the 5th duke showed the spirit of his forebears and placed himself in direct opposition to Bute and therefore also – politically – to his monarch. Enter into the arena John Wilkes, radical MP, journalist (he was editor of the *North Briton*) and rake. Wilkes used his newspaper to attack Bute and the Leicester House faction without mercy, but it was his criticism of a speech made by the king that saw him in the dock, charged with seditious libel. Bolton was prepared to 'put his money where his mouth was', and together with Richard Grenville-Temple, 2nd Earl Temple, he stood bail for the beleaguered Wilkes. Using parliamentary privilege, Wilkes was protected from further legal action and amid the uproar (Wilkes was popular with the public), Bute resigned from office. The furore still simmered at the end of the year, when Wilkes was challenged to a duel and ended up with a bullet in his belly. Upon being carried back to his house,

> instead of keeping him quiet, his friends have shown their zeal by visiting him, and himself has been all spirits and riot, and sat up in his bed the next morning to correct the press for tomorrow's *North Briton*. His bon mots are all over the town, but too gross, I think, to repeat.

Most of these 'bon mots' were at the expense of Bute's successor, Lord George Grenville, who Wilkes hated every bit as much as Bute. The friends who had rushed to Wilkes' bedside included Lord Temple and William Pitt (the Elder, later 1st Earl of Chatham), the new prime minister's brother and brother-in-law respectively, and also 'his Grace, the Duke of Bolton'. George III, seeing plots everywhere in the early years of his reign and with the fates of

John Wilkes by William Hogarth, 1763. (*Yale Center for British Art, Paul Mellon Collection*)

William Pitt the Elder, giving a speech in the House while suffering from gout. (*Yale University, Lewis Walpole Library*)

his ancestors before him (it was only just over a century since Charles I's execution), grew suspicious of Bolton and his cohorts. Bolton's lineage had given their wholehearted support to the Hanoverian dynasty, and indeed, had been unwavering to the crown since the Glorious Revolution of 1688, but now the tide had turned.[9]

Back in Hampshire, things were also getting nasty and worryingly personal. The Marquess of Carnarvon was an old adversary of Bolton, and Carnarvon, who was in full favour with the king, wrestled away the position of Lord Lieutenant of Hampshire. The historian Edward Gibbon wrote to his stepmother on 6 August 1763 to say:

> You may imagine how glad I am to hear of the fall of our tyrant and the accession of a just and righteous prince. Lord Carnarvon was always our utmost wish, and I have so very good an opinion of him as to believe he will not even plague our enemies to oblige us.[10]

Bolton now held no official position. He was in opposition to the government, out of favour with the king, and his personal life, much as he loved his unconventional family, was tainted with guilt and worry for the future happiness of Mary and her two daughters. It must have been at around this time that he made that ill-fated attempt to marry Mary Banks Brown, perhaps in the hope of an heir to secure his line and therefore also to guarantee provision for his womenfolk. Fatefully, the duke's clandestine wedding was a doomed venture, ending in the entry being 'abstracted' from the register to hide evidence of a marriage that was perhaps bigamous and unlawful. With his

George III in his coronation robes, by Joshua Reynolds. (*Brighton Pavilion & Museums, Brighton & Hove*)

mental health spiralling downwards, did the suicide of his half-brother play on the duke's mind?[11]

Bolton had one last chance to regain his status. During late August 1763, Bute attempted to entice William Pitt back into office (Pitt had resigned from his position as Leader of the House of Commons two years earlier, together with Lord Temple). Pitt was the self-imposed leader of 'the great Whig families' who formed the opposition; he was also, as it turned out, a good friend to his ally, the Duke of Bolton. Pitt declared that he and his friends 'could never come into Government but as a party', and among the conditions he laid down for returning to the government, it was asked that Bolton, already a Knight of the Bath, should receive the higher honour and become a Knight of the Garter. The negotiations came to nothing; the king thought the terms 'too hard' and Pitt turned his back on Parliament for a while. Life turns and turns about on such decisions. For Bolton, it proved to be the final straw regarding any pretensions he had to a role in public life. Two years later, still outcast to all intents and purposes, he made that fateful decision to end his life and blew his brains out in the parlour of his house in Grosvenor Square. Afterwards, Horace Walpole seemed to revel in the news of the duke's death, referencing the dispute over the chivalric orders and saying that he was 'glad [Bolton] had not a blue garter but a red one'.[12]

Beforehand, Bolton had been diligent in laying out the groundwork for his little family's future financial security. In his lengthy and carefully-worded will, written two years earlier, the duke left substantial bequests and annuities to his daughter Jean Mary, his mistress Mary Banks Brown and the girl who he viewed as a step-daughter, Mary Charlotte Thornhill More. Thinking ahead and attempting to play the long game, the duke did more than this. He left clear instructions that his brother Harry, who would be the next – and 6th – Duke of Bolton, should only be tenant-for-life of the family estates and, if Harry died without leaving a legitimate male heir to inherit, then those estates should revert to Jean Mary. He named Mary Banks Brown's brother Captain Francis Banks as one of the two executors to the will; Bolton knew that Francis would fight his sister and nieces' corner in any legal shenanigans to come.[13]

Quite possibly, this desperate but fragile wish to see his natural-born daughter one day inherit the Bolton estates was one of the myriad causes that lay behind Bolton's depression and melancholy. His younger brother, Lord Harry, had just the one surviving child from his marriage to Mary Nunn, his daughter Mary Henrietta. Assuming that Harry had no further children, a possibility that grew with each passing year, then without the 5th duke's instructions from beyond

William Cavendish, 4th Duke of Devonshire (when Marquess of Hartington), by William Hogarth, 1741. (*Yale Center for British Art, Paul Mellon Collection*)

the grave, Mary Henrietta would be the one to inherit the estates and fortune. Bolton refused to see his daughter cast into the role of 'poor relation', as his own half-brother and the three sons of the 3rd duke and Lavinia had been. The duke must have congratulated himself that, despite everything, he had paved the way for Jean Mary to gain the estates at a later date. Then Harry's wife died and, on 8 April 1765, he married again. His new wife was in her late twenties, hale and hearty and with every expectation of having children, and all of a sudden it no longer looked impossible that Harry would, after all, one day have a son. With everything falling apart around him, Bolton must have brooded on the actions of his elder half-brother, Colonel Perry. Is it any coincidence that three months later Jean Mary's father was dead?

A spurious little pamphlet was published with indecent haste once news of the duke's demise became known, titled *A Dialogue in the Elysian Fields, between two D-k-s*. Although the two dukes were named only by their initial, it was obvious to anyone reading that they were the 5th Duke of Bolton and William Cavendish, 4th Duke of Devonshire who had died in October 1764 at Spa. Within the pages of this epistle, the two dukes were represented as 'meeting in the shades' where they admitted that they had acted as the dupes of an 'atrocious faction' that had brought their country to the brink of ruin. Popular opinion, at least, blamed the duke's political difficulties for his suicide.[14]

Chapter Twelve

The Last Duke of Bolton

With his brother's sudden death, Lord Harry Powlett found himself the 6th Duke of Bolton.

Harry's career thus far, naval and political, had not been a total success. He was often embroiled in trouble; in his younger days, stung with criticism that his naval captaincy was due to nepotism rather than merit, Harry was arrogant in demonstrating his own bravery. There was plenty of action to be found on the high seas at the time, as Britain was engaged in various conflicts. The country was at war with Spain over disputed territories in the Caribbean and New Granada (known as the War of Jenkins' Ear and lasting from 1739 to 1748) and closer to home, sides were being taken in the War of the Austrian Succession. At the death of the Holy Roman Emperor Charles VI in 1740, the Austrian Habsburg lands were deep in debt; when Charles VI's daughter Maria Theresa took his place and ruled as archduchess (she was the only female Habsburg ruler), many of the other fractious rulers in the region saw their chance. As it had been in the days of the Winter King and Queen, the area was riven with disputes; their former kingdom of Bohemia was just one of the areas being fought over. The new archduchess was also Queen of Bohemia, but the man who had succeeded her father as Holy Roman Emperor and ruled as Charles VII ousted her for a time. Britain supported Maria Theresa and Austria, while France and Spain weighed in to the war to support Charles VII. (Maria Theresa's youngest daughter, born fifteen years after she became the archduchess, was Marie Antoinette, later the ill-fated Queen of France.)

In the middle of all this, a squadron of British naval ships mounted a blockade outside the port town of Toulon on France's southern coastline. Officially, Britain and France were not yet at war and French ships were allowed to come and go from the port. Some Spanish galleys that had taken refuge in Toulon were permitted no such leeway. When the galleys broke out of Toulon and made for the open sea, they were accompanied by French ships giving cover in an attempt to prevent pursuit. The British fleet gave chase nevertheless, and the subsequent ignominious action became known as the Battle of Toulon. The

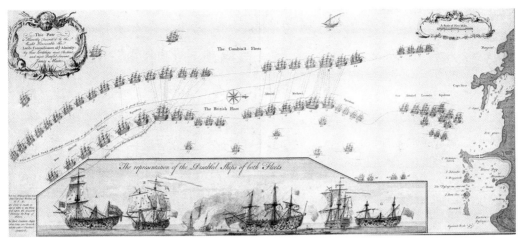

Plan of the Battle of Toulon, 1744. HMS *Oxford* was in Lestock's squadron to the right. (*Bibliothèque nationale de France*)

combined Franco-Spanish fleet inflicted heavy damage on the British naval vessels, and the latter had to retreat to Menorca and leave the Mediterranean Sea to the control of their enemies. Harry Powlett had captained one of the British ships, HMS *Oxford*, a fifty-gun fourth-rate ship of the line, but although involved in the chase, he had avoided the battle.[1]

Smarting over the defeat, and maybe wanting to cover himself in glory despite the outcome, in the court-martial that followed, Powlett gave evidence against his superior, Richard Lestock, the Vice Admiral of the White; Lestock had commanded the rear division (including HMS *Oxford*) which had arrived too late to participate in the battle and managed to transfer the blame onto the Admiral of the Blue, Thomas Mathews, but public opinion went against Lestock, even though he was acquitted.

Thomas Griffin of Goodrich Castle, Vice Admiral of the Blue and a veteran seadog, wasn't as lucky as Lestock when, in December 1750, he had to face his own four-day court-martial to answer charges of misconduct brought against him by a junior officer. That officer, somewhat predictably, was the puffed up and self-important Harry Powlett, who was convinced that Griffin's failure to engage a small squadron of French ships in action two years earlier, when in the East Indies, was due to cowardice. If he had expected to be cheered for bringing this action, Captain Powlett was misguided. Instead, by the time of Griffin's court-martial, Powlett had already been immortalized satirically by Tobias Smollett in his riotous novel *The Adventures of Roderick Random* (first published in 1748). Within the pages of the book, the eponymous hero scampers through many adventures in eighteenth-century London, and also on the high seas, aboard a privateer and then press-ganged onto a warship. There, Roderick Random meets Captain Whiffle, the ship's fey homosexual officer who had to be revived with smelling salts and a liberal sprinkling of lavender oil when the ship's surgeon's first mate came too close and overpowered Whiffle with the stench of tobacco. Contemporary readers were clearly expected to recognize Powlett in the description of the peacocking, effeminate Captain Whiffle:

> Overshadowed with a vast umbrella ... being a tall, thin young man, dressed in this manner; a white hat, garnished with a red feather, adorned his head, from whence his hair flowed upon his shoulders, in ringlets tied behind with ribbon. His coat, consisting of a pink-coloured silk, lined with white, by the elegance of the cut retired backwards, as it were, to discover a white satin waistcoat embroidered with gold, unbuttoned at the upper part to display a brooch set with garnets, that glittered in the breast of his shirt, which was of the finest cambric edged with right Mechlin: the knees of his crimson velvet breeches scarce descended so low as to meet his silk stockings, which rose without a spot or wrinkle on his meagre legs, from shoes of blue Meroquin, studded with diamond buckles that flamed forth rivals to the sun! A steel-hilted sword, inlaid with gold, and decked with a knot of ribbon which fell down in a rich tassel, equipped his side; and an amber-headed cane hung dangling from his wrist. But the most remarkable parts of his furniture were, a mask on his face, and white gloves on his hands which did not seem to be put on with an intention to be pulled off occasionally, but were fixed with a curious ring on the little finger of each hand.

Even years later, an effeminate and dandified macaroni (a man of fashion) was sometimes referred to as a 'Billy Whiffle'. Powlett had no choice in the face of such mockery but to continue in his attack on Griffin who, at the conclusion of the court-martial, was suspended from his rank. It was an ill-tempered and ugly affair that didn't end there. In a tit-for-tat exchange, Griffin retaliated by attempting to have Powlett charged with cowardice.

It was a charge of which Powlett was cleared ... eventually. The search for a witness to speak against him rumbled on for five years, and the stress and ignominy of the matter took its toll on Harry, not helped by a second

Morgan offending the delicate organs of Captain Whiffle, by Thomas Rowlandson. (*Digital Commonwealth, Massachusetts Collections Online*)

incident that saw him facing his own court-martial. In 1755, while captain of the ninety-gun HMS *Barfleur* and having become separated from the fleet off the coast of France, Harry was advised by the ship's carpenter that the vessel's stern post needed urgent repairs, and so took the decision to return to dock in England. However, the next morning, instead of joining three British men of war, he chased after a French ship before heading for Spithead to dock for the necessary repairs. There, in a stroke of bad luck for both Harry and the carpenter, it was discovered that there was no pressing need for any urgent repairs and so Captain Powlett found himself charged with abandoning the fleet and returning to port without justification. He was admonished on the former charge and cleared of the second when the carpenter took the blame. This farce

The *Barfleur*, a Second Rate, carrying 90 Guns and 680 Men, after Thomas Baston. (*Yale Center for British Art, Paul Mellon Collection*)

did nothing to mend his reputation: the press vilified him, even suggesting that Harry himself had written the carpenter's report and left the man to shoulder all the responsibility. For Harry, who now added the epithet 'Captain Sternpost' to the list of his mockeries, his reputation never recovered.[2]

Egged on by vicious attacks against both men in pamphlets and in the press, Harry Powlett and Admiral Griffin met in February 1756 to settle their differences in a duel. The match was to be held in a discreet corner of Hyde Park, but too many people turned up to watch the contest so Blackheath was proposed instead. Despite initial reports that Harry had been mortally wounded, he received nothing more than a slight injury to his hip and to one of his little fingers. The result of the duel left things inconclusive.[3]

The diarist and author Hester Lynch Thrale (later Hester Lynch Piozzi) told a funny story about Lord Harry Powlett. Harry was keen on one of Hester's friends, and the lady asked him if he could get two small monkeys for her to

Admiral Thomas Griffin.
(*National Library of Wales*)

keep as pets. Harry wrote to a friend who was an East India merchant who owed him a favour, but both his handwriting and spelling let him down. In a terrible scrawl, Harry asked for 'too monkies', which Harry's friend misread. The East India merchant thought he was being asked to find '100 monkies'. Despite private misgivings at such an astonishing request, the merchant duly set forth to fulfil it. 'What was poor Lord Harry Powlett's dismay,' wrote Hester, 'when a letter came to hand, with the news that he would receive fifty monkies by such a ship, and fifty more by the next conveyance, making up the *hundred* according to his lordship's commands!'[4]

Even though she was only in her twenties, Katherine Lowther, Harry's second wife, was old by the standards of the day at her marriage, but that was because she had been betrothed to another before Harry. Years earlier, in 1758 and at Bath, Katherine Lowther had renewed an acquaintance with Brigadier (later Major) General James Wolfe (home on leave after seeing action overseas during the Seven Years' War), and over the Christmas period she agreed to become his wife.

Hester Lynch Thrale. (*Yale Center for British Art, Paul Mellon Collection*)

The Lowthers were a wealthy family. Katherine's father, Robert Lowther, held several plantations in the Caribbean and was governor of Barbados; her brother James (known as Wicked Jimmy) was a baronet who had inherited several family estates (he would later become the 1st Earl Lonsdale). Before any wedding could take place, however, Wolfe was sent to North America to lead

James Wolfe. (*Xijky/Wikimedia Commons/PD-US/CC-BY-SA-3.0*)

the British assault on Québec City. After several weeks of inconclusive action, Wolfe led an amphibious landing of almost 4,500 men who scaled the cliffs to the Plains of Abraham and surprised the French: the battle was won by Wolfe in fifteen minutes but at huge personal cost. He was shot three times and, as

The Death of General Wolfe at Québec. (*Wellcome Library*)

he had predicted before the action, died from his injuries. Québec surrendered five days later, and Wolfe's assault was pivotal to the ending of the Seven Years' War. A miniature portrait of Katherine, which Wolfe carried with him, was returned to her. Wolfe specifically mentioned in his will that it should be set with jewels worth 500 guineas first.

Six years later Katherine married Harry Powlett (who we will now address as the duke or Bolton). Two daughters followed the marriage, Katherine Margaretta (born 28 August 1766) and Amelia (born 6 July 1768), but no sons who could inherit the dukedom. If that had been a possibility that had plagued the 5th Duke of Bolton, then he need not have worried.[5]

The new Duke of Bolton's most immediate concern was to mend relations with the king, which had been damaged almost beyond repair by his brother's support of the opposition and friendship with Wilkes. Bolton, days after learning of his brother's death, sought out John Perceval, 2nd Earl of Egmont (who was First Lord of the Admiralty). Lord Egmont wrote to the king:

> I have had lately a very long and confidential conversation with the Duke of Bolton, which I believe your Majesty will think it my duty to communicate without loss of time, as I understand that he is to attend your Majesty tomorrow. He told me frankly that his brother the late Duke had attached himself to Lord Temple & Mr Pit [*sic*] entirely by his management and at his instigation: but that both his own situation, & that of the publick are at this time entirely changed. That he considers himself now totally freed from all connexions, & for the future will avoid all engagements of that kind with any subject, or any party whatsoever. That his attachment shall be to the crown only. That he sees how contemptible, & weak it is for a Peer of England independent as he is, and with a great Estate, to be dragged along in the suite of any Private Man or set of men whatsoever, and to become the mean instrument of their views, their faction, or ambition. He gave me leave to say that these were his sentiments where I thought proper to say it, which I took as a hint to report the conversation to your Majesty & to your Majesty only. It will therefore rest in your Majesty's judgment, how far (without seeming to know anything from me) your Majesty may think fit to give him an opportunity for a like declaration of his sentiments personally to yourself, if he should wish to do so.[6]

For a time, at least, Bolton voted with the government and in return he was appointed governor of the Isle of Wight. Also around the time of his accession to the dukedom, Bolton sat for a portrait by Sir Francis Cotes which remains unfinished but which the duke accepted nonetheless. Possibly the portrait hadn't been completed at the time of Cotes' death in 1770 and Bolton's duties on the Isle of Wight had contributed to a delay in the execution of the painting.[7]

The reading of his elder brother's will precipitated several legal suits; Harry tried to contest it but to no avail. A suit in chancery was decided in 1768, and afterwards the family's old manor of Edington was sold to Peter Delmé, a wealthy banker's son who had been Southampton's MP. (In one of those curious twists of fate, Delmé also ended his life by shooting himself in his own Grosvenor Square house, located four doors further down from the 5th Duke of Bolton's former home.)[8]

Lady Katherine Powlett, after Sir Joshua Reynolds. (*Yale Center for British Art, Paul Mellon Collection*)

It is possible that Amelia, the duke's younger daughter, was born prematurely, and this may have contributed to problems with her health and wellbeing later in her life. A few weeks before her birth, Katherine, Duchess of Bolton was presiding over a glittering masked ball at Hackwood, which suggests that she hadn't yet begun to prepare for her lying-in. The 4th duke had been a doughty old widower when he came into the family estates and the 5th duke had no

Ladies Katherine and
Amelia Powlett from Daniel
Gardner, painter in pastel and
gouache; a brief account of
his life and works by Dr G.C.
Williamson, 1921.

duchess to play hostess at grand events, but now Hackwood was once more a
venue for society balls and dinners. There were 300 guests on that particular
evening, all 'of the first rank', but the dismal British weather spoiled much of
the planned spectacle. Temporary buildings had been erected in the woods,
housing a band of musicians and providing the setting for a grand supper lit
with illuminations, giving a fairy-tale-like setting reminiscent of a *fête champètre*
from days of yore. The guests, in fancy dress and with their faces hidden by
the requisite masks, would be able to dance and mingle under the stars in the
manicured garden where, in the middle of a canal and harking back to the
family's royalist steadfastness in the previous century, stood a statue of Charles
I. An immense canopy had been placed over this, forming a kind of tent which
was enclosed on three sides, leaving one side open as a grand entrance and
inside, it was intended that a multitude of lamps would provide a dazzling
light. Then the heavens opened a few hours beforehand and so a suite of six

rooms inside Hackwood were hastily prepared for the ball and supper and the outdoor festivities were abandoned. The Duchess of Bolton, despite her pregnancy, first appeared in a man's black domino and 'diverted herself some time in that manner'. Then she retired to her dressing room for a lengthy transformation and returned to her guests in the guise of a Persian princess, her gown embroidered with diamonds giving 'a magnificence that seemed truly eastern'. All in all, the duchess doesn't sound like a woman in the latter stages of pregnancy. Other people present were also richly dressed: Mrs Garrick (the German-born Eva Marie née Veigel, attending with her husband, the actor, playwright and theatre manager, David Garrick) made 'a very fine figure in a Venetian Carnival Habit' and George Montagu, 4th Duke of Manchester was dressed in sumptuous *Olde English* style, adorned with costly jewels. Lady Waldegrave and her husband, William Henry, Duke of Gloucester (George III's younger brother) left a mixed impression. While the duke wore a shabby, dirty lutestring domino, Lady Waldegrave was a graceful eastern Sultana with a profusion of jewels. (The duke and Lady Waldegrave, née Maria Walpole, had secretly married three years earlier, hence she could not appear as a duchess; the king was furious when he discovered the truth.) Leaving the finery mostly to the ladies, the Duke of Bolton's costume was a simple black domino, but it was estimated that the jewels worn by the women present at the ball were, between them, worth 270,000*l*. The guest list far exceeded the number of beds available (ahead of the ball, carriages had clogged the roads to Hackwood) and the duke paid for around 200 beds in the nearby town of Basingstoke to accommodate everyone:

> The whole company kept on their masks till about one o'clock, when they removed down to supper, to which they were conveyed through a corridor beautifully illuminated with wax lights. The entertainment did great honour to the taste of the noble hosts, and the whole evening was passed with the highest satisfaction; nor did the company part till six the next morning, all in high spirits, though the ladies seemed to complain that the Faro Bank engrossed the attention of the gentleman after supper… Upon the whole it may be justly reckoned the most elegant thing of the kind that has been seen in England for many years, and sets an example worthy of being followed by those whom fortune has enabled not only to show their taste, but to do great good in benefiting trade; an advantage, which this species of entertainment possesses above all others.[9]

David Garrick and his wife Eva Marie after William Hogarth. (*Yale Center for British Art, Paul Mellon Collection*)

Fate as well as fortune dealt its hand to the family of the 6th Duke of Bolton. While Katherine Margaretta grew up strong and healthy and made a fabulous marriage to her wealthy and titled cousin (the Duke of Cleveland's son and heir), all wasn't well with poor Amelia. Less than a month after her 17th birthday, Amelia was deemed to be – in the bald and, to our ears today, cruel terminology of the era – a lunatic. She was placed into the care of a doctor at the small and picturesque town of Petworth in West Sussex and there she remained. A commission into the extent of her mental illness carried out in

To give an idea of the intended entertainments, this is the supper room and part of the ballroom in a pavilion erected for a *fête champètre* in the Earl of Derby's garden. (*Yale Center for British Art, Paul Mellon Collection*)

June 1809 concluded that Amelia had no lucid intervals and wasn't able to make any decisions about herself or her property. All was to be administered on her behalf to the benefit of her nephew, Katherine Margaretta's eldest son Henry Vane, Viscount Barnard (later the 2nd Duke of Cleveland; he was descended from Charles II's mistress Barbara Villiers, Duchess of Cleveland). At the age of 47, Amelia died at the private institution in which she was both patient and prisoner; she was buried at Basing with her ancestors.[10]

Chapter Thirteen

Baron Bolton

Jean Mary Brown Powlett was an heiress and had the chance of inheriting the Bolton estates one day, but was unmarried in her mid-twenties. She had no-one of influence to introduce her onto the merry-go-round of the high-society marriage market. Her father was dead, and his family had no desire to see Jean Mary raised up to any great height. Mary Banks Brown, to all intents and purposes a grieving widow, was stymied by social stigma: her birth was middling and she had 'lived in sin'. The 5th Duke of Bolton might have thought that Jean Mary's uncle Captain Francis Banks would be a father figure, and perhaps he was until his death in 1777 at Newport, Rhode Island while on naval service during the American War of Independence. Francis had been ill for some time. The physician Charles Blagden was also at Newport and wrote to his friend Sir Joseph Banks to say that he 'your cousin Cap^n Banks is here, & not in a very good state of health; he was so ill in the winter, that Dr North attended him a long time.'[1]

Thomas Christopher Banks, who claimed to be Mary and Francis Banks' relation, later wrote to Sir Joseph Banks, claiming family ties with the whole extended Banks family and insisting that he, Thomas Christopher, had been named as the main beneficiary in Francis's will, and alleged that Mary had thwarted this to feather her own nest. He said that:

> A long time before Captain Francis Banks's death he borrowed money from TC Banks's father, his best friend. When great uncles Collingwood & George Banks died Francis inherited the family money and Overton Lead Mines. Whatever money he had when he died it was meant for me. He made his will before he sailed for America and he gave me the whole of what he had to leave, but the severe stroke he received in being arrested at Portsmouth on the eve of sailing preyed on his mind (with the trouble he had left my father in) that he died of a broken heart. But that event while it left my father under heavy engagements to pay, both for him, Mrs Williams deprived our family of all the benefit of the

will he had made which was destroyed by his sister Mrs Brown, to take
possession of his effects, to indemnify herself at the expense of my father
and me. It was Jean Mary who was to ensure that my father & I were
repaid the monies loaned by Francis, but she decided not to do this.

Given their obvious closeness, would Francis leave his fortune to anyone other
than his sister and her two daughters? No will for Francis has yet been discovered
and if he was ill and sailing the high seas on active service, it seems incredible
that he would not have written one. Perhaps, after all, Mary Banks Brown did
destroy her brother's will so that she could take control of his effects?

Captain Banks' death left Jean Mary adrift. She was 26 years of age and still
single. That changed when she met Thomas Orde, a handsome gentleman from
Morpeth in Northumberland. On 7 April 1778, at St Marylebone Church,
Jean Mary Brown Powlett walked up the aisle to marry him, with the blessing
of her mother. Standing witness to the marriage was Mary Charlotte Williams,
Jean Mary's elder half-sister who had herself married some years earlier to John
Williams, a West Indian planter. The second witness was Thomas Orde's close
friend, Thomas Villiers, Lord Hyde (later the 2nd Earl of Clarendon).[2]

Thomas was the son of the county magistrate and landowner John Orde by
his second wife Anne. Educated at Eton and then at King's College, Cambridge
(where he gained a Master of Arts), Thomas Orde departed for the continent
on that traditional jaunt of well-to-do young men, the Grand Tour. A talented
amateur artist, Thomas always had a sketch book with him, judging from the
wealth of etchings, watercolours and cartoons which have survived, many
drawn from life. Several were published. While on a visit to the spa town of
Buxton in Derbyshire, shortly before his marriage, Thomas took the likeness
of the 20-year-old Georgiana Cavendish, Duchess of Devonshire.[3]

After his marriage, Thomas stood for Parliament, representing Aylesbury in
Buckinghamshire and then Harwich in Essex, and official positions followed;
he was appointed to the Privy Council as Chief Secretary for Ireland and
as Secretary to the Treasury. The Irish position, as secretary to the Lord
Lieutenant of Ireland, the Duke of Rutland, proved particularly troublesome,
occurring during the ministry of William Pitt and at a time when the British
government was trying to push through a policy of closer union between the
two countries. Tension arose when the British ministers wanted Ireland to pay
an annual financial contribution against the promise of generous trade deals.
Thomas Orde, often unwell, found himself caught in the middle, trying to
present Irish interests to the government in Westminster and vice versa. As he

Newport, Rhode Island. (*New York Public Library*)

explained himself in a letter to Pitt defending his lack of success in securing the government's objectives, he was 'in a perpetual scene of warfare both on the one side and on the other'. Pitt suggested to Rutland that he should dismiss Orde, but the duke stood firm and persuaded the prime minister of Orde's abilities. Dublin was in a state of unrest, and Orde's greatest success in Ireland (in the eyes of the British) was the establishment of a police force controlled by the government, an initiative personally overseen by him. The Duke of Rutland's early death saw the end of Thomas Orde's tenure as Chief Secretary for Ireland, and one gets the impression that Thomas was heartily glad to return to his English estates, his wife and family, notwithstanding his sorrow at losing a friend and patron. Thanks to Jean Mary's influence and his connection with one of the great landed families of Hampshire, Thomas was made governor of the Isle of Wight in 1791, a position that he held for more than fifteen years, but even this wasn't without its difficulties. Jean Mary's uncle Harry, the 6th duke, had been forced to step down from the governorship of the Isle of Wight to make way for Thomas Orde, a situation that reinforced the ill-feeling building

Thomas Orde's parents, John and Anne Orde, watching William Orde's return from Shooting, by Arthur Devis, 1754–56. (William was Thomas Orde's older half-brother). (*Yale Center for British Art, Paul Mellon Collection*)

up within the family as both sides jostled for position. High in favour with the current administration, Orde held the upper hand over the duke who had fallen foul of ministers who held sway in Parliament. For the duke, the loss of the income the governorship brought with it was more than compensated for by the reinstatement of his naval pension of 4,000*l*. a year. Harry hadn't been able to claim this while he was governor and it was, as the newspapers pointed out, a further drain on the public purse. Moreover, it was a public declaration of the ministry and crown's favour of Thomas Orde, to the detriment of the duke.[4]

Thomas Orde was wealthy and life was more than comfortable financially for the couple (during the lifetime of the 6th duke, Orde received a pension on the

Georgiana, Duchess of Devonshire, sketched by Thomas Orde at Buxton in 1777. (*North Yorkshire County Record Office*)

Irish Establishment of 1,700*l.* a year). All the time, however, there was one eye on the Bolton estates where Jean Mary's uncle Harry, the 6th Duke of Bolton lived. With no son and heir to follow him and time running out for one to be born, in accordance with the watertight last will and testament so carefully drawn up by Jean Mary's father, upon the death of the 6th duke Thomas and Jean Mary Orde would inherit. During this time, the Ordes had five children (three more had died in infancy): three sons – William, Thomas and Charles – and two daughters – Mary Jean and Anne – so the Ordes' succession in the male line looked secure. The relationships between the two families must have been fraught in the extreme.

Jean Mary's half-sister hadn't been so fortunate. The case in Chancery brought by the 6th Duke of Bolton to contest the will had returned a less favourable verdict for Mary Charlotte than that issued down to Jean Mary. To compensate for this, Jean Mary had issued bonds allowing the Williamses to procure credit against the expectation of Jean Mary inheriting the Bolton

Volunteers receiving the Isle of Wight banner from Thomas Orde-Powlett, 1798. (*Yale Center for British Art, Paul Mellon Collection*)

estates, although her mother had counselled against it. Mary Banks Brown had the measure of her son-in-law and could see that John Williams was a spendthrift and, it seems, something of a wastrel. For a while, the Williamses kept up an appearance of genteel respectability; John Williams was elected as MP for Saltash in Cornwall and he, Mary Charlotte and their two children (Sarah Charlotte and John) lived on an estate to which he was entitled at Cranborne. However, amid recriminations, arguments and money worries, in 1777 the Cranborne estate was sold to pay the mounting debts (John Williams' affairs had become 'wholly deranged') and once he'd milked Jean Mary of as much as he could, Williams left his marital home and took a mistress, Anna Maria Thompson. Mary Charlotte had no-one but her sister Jean Mary to turn to for help; their mother, Mary Banks Brown, died in 1782.[5]

The Ordes took in Mary Charlotte Williams' two young children, raising them alongside their own growing family and paying the school fees for Mary Charlotte's son. Meanwhile, the scapegrace John Williams relocated to the Bristol area with Anna Maria and had two further children, Frances Herbert and Charles Shutter Williams, before sailing back to his family's plantation on the islands of Grenada and Nevis. When Williams died in 1792 his will (for what it was worth because he left debts on an enormous scale) didn't mention his wife at all and simply bequeathed everything to his children, both legitimate and illegitimate, and to Anna Maria.[6]

Having brought up the two Williams children, Thomas and Jean Mary must have despaired when John, at 21 years of age, married the daughter of a sedan chairman, a woman with a dubious history. Charlotte Goulding, a couple of years younger than John, was the niece of the infamous Laetitia (Letty) Lade, who had provided London with a rich source of scandal. Popular gossip said that Letty had once been in love with a notorious highwayman, John 'Sixteen String Jack' Rann and lived as his mistress. An affair with the Prince of Wales's younger brother Frederick, Duke of York was also rumoured. Working-class and from the slums of London's rookeries, it was Letty's skill in the saddle as much as her wanton beauty that catapulted her into the echelons of high society. Sir John Lade, a disreputable man of the turf, fell for her and made Letty his wife. As Lady Lade, Letty became a favourite of the prince, despite her propensity for swearing like a trooper. Letty introduced her pretty niece Charlotte Goulding to her friends, and one of those friends was Richard Barry, 7th Earl of Barrymore. Nicknamed Hellgate and every bit as notorious as Sir John Lade, Barry eloped with Charlotte. It wasn't a wise move by Charlotte: Barry was up to his eyeballs in debt and, to pay them, he took a commission in the Royal Berkshire Militia. While escorting French prisoners of war from Rye to Deal in a gig, Barry's musket discharged accidentally, killing him stone dead and leaving the young Lady Barrymore an 18-year-old widow. Just over a year later, Charlotte married John Williams who had been commissioned a captain in the 3rd Foot Guards.[7]

On Christmas Day 1794, while celebrating with his family at Hackwood, Harry Powlett died. In contrast to the lengthy legal document left by his elder brother, his own will was short and to the point. He didn't try to contest the one left by his brother or attempt to subvert it, but simply stipulated that all his personal wealth and estate should pass to his wife. More than likely, he had been converting what he could of the estate's income into personal property, planning for the future maintenance of his wife and daughters. The Duchess of Bolton often appeared dressed in a very extravagant and costly style; in 1770 she was reported to have been adorned with jewels estimated to be worth 40,000*l.* (about £3.5 million in today's money) when attending court, and she eclipsed the other ladies. With Bolton's death, Thomas Orde's 1,700*l.* a year pension

The Accomplished Sportswoman: engraving of Lady Laetitia Lade from the *Sporting Magazine*, June 1794.

Hackwood Park, c.1818. (*British Library: Flickr*)

ceased, but this was of no concern to him; his wife had now come into the instant possession of an estate worth 17,000*l*. per annum, ten times the sum they forfeited.[8]

Katherine, now the Dowager Duchess of Bolton, had no choice but to vacate Hackwood and Bolton Hall. Thomas Orde moved quickly and within two weeks of Harry's demise he had added the additional surname of Powlett to his own (by Royal Licence), creating a double-barrelled surname that the family uses to this day: Orde-Powlett. The one thing lacking was a title because the dukedom could not pass to Jean Mary who was debarred by the double hammer blow of being a

The novelist Jane Austen. (*British Library: Flickr*)

female of illegitimate birth. After 105 years, there was no 7th Duke of Bolton and the title fell into abeyance. The lesser title, Marquess of Winchester, went sideways to a distant relation, George Paulet, a great-grandson of the 4th Marquess of Winchester and a descendant of the Powletts of Amport House in Hampshire (Paulet became the 12th Marquess of Winchester, in its reversion). Two years later, King George III addressed the issue of rank and created Thomas Orde-Powlett the 1st Baron Bolton of Bolton Castle in the County of York. Jean Mary, like her mother before her, was never a duchess but she was now Lady Bolton, the evocative title still harking back to Mary Scrope and the castle she brought into the family more than a century earlier.

Lord and Lady Bolton now moved among the most aristocratic of Hampshire society, an irony – given their births – that wasn't lost on the novelist Jane Austen. The two families, Orde-Powlett and Austen, were often present at the same social gatherings and the former didn't escape Jane's often caustic wit. In mid-December 1798 she ended a letter written from her father's rectory in the village of Steventon to her sister Cassandra by saying that 'Lord Bolton is particularly curious in his pigs, has had pigstyes of a most elegant construction built for them, and visits them every morning as soon as he rises.' Two years later, after a ball where they had all been present, Jane observed that Lady Bolton was 'much improved by a wig'.

Jane Austen also knew Charles Powlett, grandson of the 3rd Duke of Bolton and Lavinia Fenton (he was Percy's son). He lived in their Hampshire neighbourhood, and Charles and his wife provided inspiration for Jane's novels: 'Charles Powlett gave a dance on Thursday, to the great disturbance of all his neighbours, of course, who, you know, take a most lively interest in the state of his finances, and live in hopes of his being soon ruined.'[9]

Brought up at Hackwood, as an adult Charles fell between two worlds: gentry and aristocracy. He aspired to the latter, but was struggling to even maintain a foothold in the former. He was known as a spendthrift. The account books of a Hampshire furniture and household wares emporium, Ring Brothers of Basingstoke where the Powletts, the Austens and all the local society families shopped, contains a curious little tale referring back to this period:

> Once there were two young men, both of them beginning clergymen, who ran up bills at Ring Brothers of Basingstoke far beyond the normal 'brought on's' expected of men in their modest line of life. These two young men, one named James Austen, the eldest brother of the famous author, and the other, Charles Powlett, the man who wanted to kiss her, met very different fates. Ring Brothers stopped Charles in mid-shopping spree by cancelling his credit, whereas James was allowed to spend double the amount. The Ring brothers had sound reasons for what they did.[10]

Before he married, Charles had been one of Jane's admirers, even asking if he could kiss her, but Jane wasn't interested in him. Months later, Charles, who took Holy Orders and thereafter held numerous livings within the gift of the (Orde-)Powlett family, married a clergyman's daughter instead, Anne (Nancy) Temple. Jane scorned the socially-ambitious Mrs Powlett: 'she is discovered to be everything that the Neighbourhood could wish her, silly & cross, as well as extravagant.' A few years later, while dining at the Powletts' rectory, Jane thought Nancy 'at once expensive and nakedly dress'd and gossip on the evening concerned the probably astronomical cost of her scanty lace and muslin gown'. The couple may well appear in Jane Austen's *Emma*. Mr Elton, the clergyman who thinks himself a suitable suitor for the eponymous heroine in the novel does appear to be a veiled description of the Reverend Charles Powlett, and the beautiful, wealthy but superficial and somewhat vulgar woman who the Reverend Elton subsequently married mirrors Powlett's wife. Nancy Powlett had a habit of referring to her husband as her *caro sposo*, an affectation that Jane gave to Mrs Elton in *Emma*.[11]

Carisbrooke Castle on the Isle of Wight, by Frederick Calvert. (*Yale Center for British Art, Paul Mellon Collection*)

Thomas Orde-Powlett was plagued by ill health and retired from public office. Instead, he devoted himself to his estates and to his family and was often in the company of his two beautiful daughters at balls and on excursions; they were the apples of his eye. Lord and Lady Bolton were grief-stricken when both their daughters died young (in their early twenties). Anne, the younger daughter, died in 1804 at Hackwood Park, and Mary Jean, the elder, less than three years later at Exmouth. In the same year, Charles, the family's youngest son, died at Carisbrooke Castle on the Isle of Wight aged just 13. The remaining two sons, William and Thomas, did live long lives and marry, but only Thomas had the necessary son and heir to succeed to the title of Baron Bolton.[12]

Mary Charlotte, Lady Bolton's elder sister, continued to be a thorn in the side of the Orde-Powletts' domesticity. She made a second marriage to a man named John Bindley, whose interest was piqued by Mary Charlotte's rich relations. Perhaps it was the trials her first husband put her through with his financial problems and desertion of her for another woman, or maybe Mary Charlotte had inherited a streak of her father Zachary Harnage More's wildness,

The ruins of Bolton Castle, LNER poster. (*Authors' own collection*)

but towards the end of the eighteenth century the family became concerned about the state of her mental health. John Bindley moved to take control of her affairs and Lord Bolton grew exasperated at Mr and Mrs Bindley's demands upon his wife's fortune.

The (Orde-)Powlett family had negotiated the reigns of nine monarchs and the interruption of the monarchy during the Commonwealth period, their fortunes fluctuating along with the crown. Jean Mary, Lady Bolton lived until the Regency, when George III's repeated bouts of madness necessitated that his eldest son rule in his stead. By that time, her eldest son William was the 2nd Baron Bolton.[13]

To the present day, the descendants of Thomas and Jean Mary Orde-Powlett carry the title Baron Bolton and still own the castle that inspired the name of the peerage. The ruins of Bolton Castle are now a fascinating visitor attraction (it is one of the country's best-preserved medieval castles).

Notes

Chapter One
1. The 5th Duke of Bolton lived at No. 32 Grosvenor Square.
2. In 1762 John Truesdale of Truesdale, Partridge and Halifax had been appointed one of two Apothecaries to the Person by George III. When the 5th Duke of Bolton wrote a codicil to his will, dated 3 October 1764, he left a substantial annuity to his housekeeper Eleanor Carter in recompense for her long service. National Archives (NA), PROB 11/910/167, Will of the most noble Charles, Duke of Bolton, of St George Hanover Square, Middlesex.
3. The Duke of Cumberland never completely recovered from a leg wound received at the Battle of Dettingen in 1743 and in later years grew increasingly obese; he suffered a stroke in 1760 and died on 31 October 1765, just a few months after the Duke of Bolton's decease.
4. *Additional Grenville Papers, 1763–1765.* Grenville was only to be prime minister for a few more days; he was dismissed from office in July 1765 by George III. Thomas Villiers had been granted the title of Baron Hyde on 3 June 1756 and was later created the 1st Earl of Clarendon, both titles in their second creation.
5. Ibid.
6. *The Grenville Papers: being the correspondence of Richard Grenville Earl Temple, K.G., and the Right Hon: George Grenville, their friends and contemporaries*, vol. 3.
7. *Letters of Horace Walpole, Earl of Orford to Sir Horace Mann, his Britannic Majesty's Resident at the court of Florence*, from 1760 to 1785, vol. 1.
8. Isabella Montagu, the dowager Duchess of Manchester, married Edward Hussey-Montagu in 1743, three years after the Earl of Scarborough's suicide.
9. *Zoonomia* by Erasmus Darwin, vol. 2, part 2.
10. *Manchester Mercury*, 16 July 1765
11. The burial took place on 10 July 1765.

Chapter Two
1. Martha Janes' surname is also recorded as Jones, James and Jeanes, and is occasionally noted as San(d)ford.
2. The description of the castle that stood at Langar comes from Leland, reprinted in Thoroton's *History of Nottinghamshire*. The village of Langar was decimated by plague in 1665 and the old castle largely abandoned and then demolished to be replaced, during the eighteenth century, with a new house, Langar Hall. Today, Langar Hall is a luxury hotel. Margaret Tybotot, wife of Roger, 2nd Baron Scrope of Bolton, was the heiress of Langar.
3. Henry Carey's mother Mary was Anne Boleyn's elder sister and had enjoyed the attentions of Henry VIII (he even named a ship after her, the *Mary Boleyn*, in 1532) before his eye settled on Anne. The affair between Henry VIII and Mary took

place after the latter's marriage to William Carey although – despite many rumours to the contrary – it appears to have ended before she became pregnant with her son. Scrope's Catholic leanings did at times play to his advantage; in 1619 he was appointed lord president of the council in the north, a position he probably owed to the Spanish ambassador (Gondomar) and the fact that James I's foreign policy at the time was supportive of the Spanish.

4. Lady Katherine Manners' two brothers had died in childhood, and their father, Francis Manners, 6th Earl of Rutland, held a local woman, Joan Flower and her two daughters, Margaret and Philippa, responsible, accusing them of witchcraft; the three women became known as the Witches of Belvoir.

5. Elizabeth was baptised (as Elizabeth Sanford) on 1 October 1627 and Annabella (as Annabella Sanford) on 18 April 1629. Emanuel Scrope, 11th Baron Bolton was created 1st Earl of Sunderland on 19 June 1627. The settlement of his property was dated 20 May 1629: see DDCC/133/21, Inspeximus by Letters Patent of a Settlement, East Yorkshire Archives. It is not clear where Martha's alias of San(d)ford originates, but there were Janes' resident in Granborough and the surrounding area of Buckinghamshire at the time. A Moses Janes is later associated with Martha in public records, clearly a relative, and so it seems most likely that she was born Martha Janes, but it remains to be established if San(d)ford denotes a marriage made at some point or whether it was an assumed surname, perhaps simply employed by Emanuel to obfuscate Martha's true parentage and birth.

6. *Maladies & Medicine: Exploring Health & Healing, 1540-1740* by Jennifer Evans and Sara Read. If Emanuel Scrope had heeded his friends' advice, he had two of the best physicians the city of London could offer as neighbours on St Martin's Lane. On one side of his London house lived the royal physician, Sir Théodore Turquet de Mayerne, and on the other, Gideon DeLaune, the King's apothecary (both men were Huguenot refugees). Richard Nappier (or Napier) had been a pupil of the astrologer and occultist, Simon Foreman.

7. Howell gives no date for Emanuel Scrope's football injury and his fortuitous pipe of tobacco administered at Belvoir Castle; the Earl of Rutland in question could either be Roger Manners, the 5th earl (who died in 1612) or his younger brother Francis, the 6th earl. Lord Willoughby is possibly one of the Baron Willoughbys of Parnham; the 3rd baron, who died 1617, married Frances Manners, the Countess of Sunderland's sister.

8. The settlement, leaving his unentailed lands to his illegitimate son, John, was dated 20 May 1629. For information on the children being placed in the custody of the Earl of Holland, see WYL100/L/31, West Yorkshire Archive Service. The Howe tomb is in the south transept of Langar Church and, at the time of writing, is closed off to public access, the area around it being used as something of a storeroom.

9. James I's eldest son Henry, Prince of Wales, died at the age of 18 in his father's lifetime, leaving Charles the heir to the throne. Besides Henry, Charles and Elizabeth there were three further daughters and a son who all died in infancy.

10. Karl Ludwig's name is Anglicized as Charles Louis. Rupert's gaoler was Count von Kuffstein and his pretty daughter was named Susan.

11. Peter Robert Newman, in volume 2 of *The Royalist Army in Northern England 1642–45* (PhD thesis, University of York) suggests that John Scrope may be one and the same as the Lieutenant Colonel James [*sic*] of the Bolton Garrison who

held that rank under Henry Chaytor. Colonel John Scrope was also known by his mother's surnames of Janes and San(d)ford.

12. News dated Tuesday, 11 November reported in *Perfect Passages of Each Dayes Proceedings in Parliament*, 5-12 November 1645. In 1761, the north-east tower, damaged during the siege, collapsed but the rest of Bolton Castle survives as a tourist attraction and is still owned by the family. John Scrope was buried on 31 July 1646.

13. Henry Carey, 1st Baron Hunsdon of Hunsdon's had sixteen children (plus several natural-born offspring); Henry Carey, Lord Leppington traced his line from Hunsdon via a younger son Robert Carey, who became the 1st Earl of Monmouth (1560–1639). Howe and his family's Royalist sympathies were rewarded at the Restoration when his father was given a baronetcy and his wife Annabella was legitimized, gaining the rank and privilege of an earl's daughter. In 1695, the fourth son of John Grubham Howe and Annabella, Emanuel Scrope Howe married Ruperta, the illegitimate daughter of the Royalist cavalier Prince Rupert of the Rhine and the seventeenth-century Drury Lane actress Margaret (Peg) Hughes. Ruperta was born in 1673.

14. One of Martha's Buckinghamshire properties was Biggin Farm, located at the bridge joining the Granborough and Winslow fields, a property tenanted by a man named Stephen Janes (clearly a relative) in the 1630s. In 1677, Martha conveyed Hambleden Manor to Sir Robert Clayton and John Morris for £4,119 3s. 4d. A son had been born to Henry, Lord Leppington and Mary, named Henry for his father, but he did not live many years and was buried on 24 May 1653 with his forebears in Westminster Abbey. Nothing now remains of the dower house in Epperstone.

Chapter Three

1. James Howell, before becoming Emanuel Scrope's secretary, had tutored Jane Savage and her siblings. He too left behind plaudits to both her brains and beauty. Both Jane and Lady Honora de Burgh were daughters of prominent Catholic noblemen.

2. The branch of the family that held the Bolton dukedom descends in this line from a Sir John Paulet who died in 1391, via his younger son William Paulet of Melcomb Paulet in Somersetshire, a serjeant at law.

3. *Mercurius Britanicus Communicating the Affaires of Great Britaine*, 18-25 November 1644.

4. Hugh Peter (or Peters) had been present at the final storming of Basing House and tried to argue the Marquess of Winchester into a denial of his royalism. Katharine Haswell later petitioned Charles II for a position for her husband. She recounted that, after many services in carrying letters, she was dangerously wounded at Basing House and disabled from a livelihood. Calendar of State Papers, Domestic Series, 1665–1665: Reign: Charles II: Entry Number: VOL. CXIII., 123: Page Number: 228: Document Ref.: SP 29/113 f.173: Date: Feb.? 1664–5.

5. *Perfect Diurnall of Some Passages in Parliament*, 12-19 January 1646.

6. National Archives, Parliamentary Archives, House of Lords: Journal Office: Main Papers 1509-1700, 61/HL/PO/JO/10/1/318.

Chapter Four

1. Colonel Adrian Scrope was descended from Henry Scrope, 6th Baron Scrope of Bolton.
2. Sarah, Lady Frescheville was the daughter and heir of Sir John Harrington. She was largely responsible for ruining the Frescheville family with her excesses. Sarah died months after her husband had been granted his barony.
3. William II, Prince of Orange, died on 6 November 1650.
4. In 1661, Henriette Anne was married to Louis XIV's younger brother, Philippe, Duke of Orléans; Phillipe's second wife was Elizabeth of the Palatine, the daughter of Prince Rupert's elder brother, Karl Ludwig who had been restored to some of his father's estates as Elector Palatine.
5. In the parish register, the marriage is entered old style, 12 February 1654. The interregnum was the period in English history from the execution of Charles I in 1649 to the Restoration of Charles II in 1660; it is also known as the Commonwealth period when England and Wales, joined later by Ireland and Scotland, were ruled as a republic. Hampshire Archives: 10M57/D13, Brief between Lord St John, against the Lord Marquess of Winchester, c.1661.
6. Francis Nicholson died in London 1728; claims that he was knighted are false. The manor of Downholme, where Nicholson was born, was owned by Mary, Lady St John and – in 1654 – she leased it to Henry Frankland Esq., the younger step-brother of the Royalist Anthony Frankland of Ellerton Abbey. Oliver Cromwell's daughter Mary, Viscountess Faucounberg, whose husband, Thomas Belasyse, Viscount (and later 1st Earl) Faucounberg was connected to the Franklands, mentioned Francis Nicholson in a letter to Henry Frankland's relative, Sir William Frankland: 'Capt. Nicholson, who was Lady Winchester's page, has been twice through Mora-tania [*sic*] as far as Mount Atlas, and is now returning again thither.' Letter dated 5 May 1683; Notes and Queries, Oxford University Press, 1903. Sir William Frankland was a member of the extended Frankland family. Clearly, Nicholson was a man well-known to both families and his career of interest to them. Further patronage came from John Egerton, 3rd Earl of Bridgewater who married Powlett's eldest daughter, Jane.

Chapter Five

1. The bodies of General Henry Ireton, Cromwell's son-in-law and John Bradshaw who had been the judge at Charles I's trial were also posthumously executed along with Cromwell.
2. Frances Stuart, later the Duchess of Richmond, was the face for Britannia, the figure used on British coinage into the early twenty-first century.
3. Mary was born c.1659 and Charles, the future 2nd Duke of Bolton, in 1661. Despite adhering to Parliament, Charles Rich, 4th Earl of Warwick and Thomas Belasyse, 1st Earl Fauconberg both supported Charles II at the Restoration. Frances Rich, née Cromwell later married Sir John Russell, 3rd Baronet. Robert Rich's father, Robert Rich, 3rd Earl of Warwick, supported the king during the Civil Wars, illustrating the divisions that occurred within families.
4. The next owner of Winchester House, from 1685, was George Holman who was the 5th Marquess of Winchester's brother-in-law; Holman's wife was Anastasia Howard, the sister of the marquess's third and final wife, Isabella. Both Howard

women were the daughters of William Howard, 1st Viscount Stafford. Sandwich was sent to Spain as an ambassador to avoid a looming scandal when he was accused of financial irregularities relating to the capture of Dutch merchant ships. Prince Rupert and the Earl of Albermarle took joint command of the navy towards the beginning of 1666. Real tennis was the forerunner of the game we know as tennis today.

5. *Samuel Pepys' Diary*, Wednesday, 30 August 1665. Elizabeth was born probably c.1664.

Chapter Six

1. Charles Berkeley, 1st Earl of Falmouth had been a staunch ally of Charles II. Married only a year earlier, his widow would become one of the king's mistresses. Charles MacCarty, Viscount Muskerry was the son of the 1st Earl of Clancarty and Richard Boyle was the son of the 1st Earl of Burlington (in its first creation).

2. Lord William Powlett was born on 14 August 1666.

3. Bramshill House is what is known as a 'prodigy house', a term for houses built by courtiers or wealthy landowners, mainly between 1570 and 1620, which were overly grandiose and showy.

4. *Samuel Pepys' Diary*, Thursday, 29 November 1666. The incident had happened a day or two earlier.

5. The Battle of Solebay took place on 7 June 1672 off the Suffolk coastline.

6. *London Gazette*, 6-9 September 1669.

7. Dudley Bard was born in 1666.

8. The 5th Marquess of Winchester died on 5 March 1675 and was buried at Englefield. NA PROB 11/347/336, Will of John Lord St John of Bazing Earl of Wiltshire and Marquess of Winchester. Honora, Marchioness of Winchester, had died in 1661 aged 51. Lord Francis Powlett and Anne had several children; their son, another Francis, and daughter Anne (wife of the Reverend Nathan Wright) successively inherited Englefield. In a 1695 list of Englefield inhabitants, a Mrs Breamore appears directly after Lord and Lady Powlett at the top of the list; this is possibly Anne's mother. (www.englefieldhistory.net)

9. *Faithful Mercury*, 22 July 1679.

10. *Calendar of the State Papers Preserved in the Public Record Office*: January 1, 1679-August 31, 1680 (HM Stationery Office, 1915). Margaret, Countess of Wiltshire, died on 7 February 1682. Charles Powlett's second marriage to Frances Ramsden took place on 8 February 1683. Earl of Wiltshire is one of the oldest titles in the peerage of England and, in 1551, had been bestowed on William Paulet, Baron St John, who afterwards became the 1st Marquess of Winchester. It is thought that the family believed the Wiltshire earldom had been surrendered when the marquessate was created, and so the heir to the title used Baron St John in the meantime. In fact, the heir to the Marquess of Wiltshire should have always used the title Earl of Wiltshire, and Charles Powlett, the future 2nd Duke of Bolton, was the first to adopt the title as his own.

11. The Palmes family of Naburn Hall are descended from Mary Boleyn via her daughter Catherine who is thought to be the natural daughter of Henry VIII, conceived while Mary was his mistress. Mary and her better-known sister Anne's

father, Thomas Boleyn was the 1st Earl of Wiltshire, but by the late 1600s the earldom was used as the courtesy title of the Marquess of Winchester's eldest son.
12. Mary, Marchioness of Winchester, was buried in Wensley Church on 12 November 1680.
13. *Memoirs of Sir John Reresby* (extract relating to the 6th Marquess of Winchester was dated August 1687).

Chapter Seven
1. Six children had been born to the Duke and Duchess of York, but all except Mary and Anne had died young. Lady Rachel Wriothesley's first husband had been Francis Vaughan, eldest son of Richard Vaughan, 2nd Earl of Carbery; Francis died young and there were no surviving children. Francis's brother John became the 3rd Earl of Carbery, and John's daughter Anne became the ill-fated wife of Charles Powlett, 3rd Duke of Bolton.
2. 'Yorkshire Politics, 1658–1688', a thesis submitted for the Degree of Doctor of Philosophy by Cheryl Margaret Keen, August 1990 (University of Sheffield, Department of History). The Dowager Lady Middleton, née Martha Carey, was the daughter of Henry Carey, 2nd Earl of Monmouth and the younger sister of Mary Scrope's first husband, Henry Carey, Lord Leppington. To 'cry peccavi' was to admit one's guilt.
3. *London Gazette*, 22 March 1683. 'Lincoln's Inn Fields: Nos. 59 and 60 (Lindsey House)' in *Survey of London: Volume 3, St Giles-in-The-Fields*, Pt I: Lincoln's Inn Fields, eds W. Edward Riley and Laurence Gomme (London, 1912). British History Online. Early Modern Letters Online (Bodleian, Oxford): MS Lister 3 fols. 189-190, 27 April 1683: Powlett (Paulet), Charles (London, England) to Lister, Martin.
4. *Calendar of the State Papers Preserved in the Public Record Office*: October 1, 1683-April 30, 1684 (HM Stationery Office, 1938).
5. Catherine Sedley, Countess of Dorchester later married Sir David Colyear, Baronet, the future Earl of Portmore. By James II, Catherine had a daughter, Lady Catherine Darnley.
6. *Calendar of the State Papers Preserved in the Public Record Office*: May 1, 1684-February 5, 1685 (HM Stationery Office, 1938) and Calendar of the State Papers Preserved in the Public Record Office: Feb-Dec 1685 (HM Stationery Office, 1960). North Yorkshire County Record Office (NYCRO), Powlett Papers, ZBO VIII.
7. By Eleanor Needham, the Duke of Monmouth also had a daughter, Isabel, who died young.
8. One of the king's regiments at the Battle of Sedgemoor was the Tangier Regiment (later the Queen's Royal West Surrey Regiment), commanded by Percy Kirke. Francis Nicholson, the Marquess of Winchester's (later 1st Duke of Bolton's) disputed illegitimate son was an officer within that regiment. Under Kirke's orders, the men were ruthless in hunting down Monmouth's defeated men following the battle.
9. The family's eldest child was Mary, born on 20 October 1683, probably at Bolton Hall as she was christened on 25 November at Wensley; she must have been conceived almost on the wedding night. Charles Powlett, the future 3rd Duke of

Bolton, was born on 3 September 1685. Both Scroop and Thomas Powlett were christened at St Martin-in-the-Fields, Westminster; Scroop on 14 November 1687 and Thomas (who was born on 13 April 1690) on 4 May 1690. Harry, the youngest son, was born on 24 July 1691.

10. Queen Anne's letter dated 20 March 1688 to her sister Mary, Princess of Orange, Ellis Correspondence, volume 1. Sir Stephen Fox was the grandfather of the Georgian Whig statesman Charles James Fox. Jane Fox married George Compton, 4th Earl of Northampton, a man much more to her family's satisfaction. The Earldom of Sunderland in its second creation was bestowed on Henry Spencer, 3rd Baron Spencer of Wormleighton in 1643 by a grateful King Charles I in recognition of Spencer's services during the Civil Wars. It was reported that gaining the title cost Henry Spencer a vast sum of money, and his fealty to his king ultimately cost him his life, at the age of 22, when he was hit by a cannonball during a battle. Both the current Duke of Marlborough and also Earl Spencer can trace their ancestry back to Robert Spencer, 2nd Earl of Sunderland.

11. The duel between Robert, Lord Spencer and Odet Fabry took place on 22 October 1684, on the Rue de la Taconnerie. Fabry left Geneva afterwards but was brought back to face justice. Lord Spencer escaped any retribution as the authorities largely turned a blind eye to the antics of a foreign gentleman. *Duels en Pays romands, XVIème-XVIIème siècles by C. Vuilleumier from Colloque LE DUEL et le combat singulier en Suisse romande, colloque du 7 au 8 mai 2010.*

12. NYCRO, Powlett Papers, ZBO VIII. From the registers of York Minster: The Right Honorable ye Lady Mary Jenkings was bur. ye 16th of March, 1689… Elizabeth ye Daughter of Mr. Tobias Jenkens was bur. the 20th of January, 1690.

13. NYCRO, Powlett Papers, ZBO VIII. The current Dukes of Norfolk and Westminster both trace their descent back to Scroop Egerton, and therefore to the 1st Duke of Bolton and Mary Scrope and their forebears.

14. While Robert, Lord Spencer's death is often given as 5 September 1688, the *Histoire Abrege'e de l'Europe pour le mois de Septembre 1688* (published the same year) gives it as 15 September: *Mylord Spencer fils ainé du Comte de Sunderland, Ministre & Secrétaire d'Etat & Président du Conseil Privé en Angleterre mourut à Paris le quinzieme Septembre, aprés une longue maladie.* Converting the date from the old into the new style, the date of Robert, Lord Spencer's death is 25 September 1688. At the coronation of William and Mary (11 April 1689) Lady Elizabeth Powlett, still unmarried, was one of the women who carried the queen's train (along with Lady Diana Vere, Lady Elizabeth Cavendish and Lady Harriot Hyde). *The History of England: During the Reigns of King William and Queen Mary, Queen Anne, King George I. Being the Sequel of the Reigns of the Stuarts* by Mr Oldmixon, 1735.

15. *The Secret History of Europe: Treating of the following particulars: of the Duke of Monmouth's reception at The Hague by the States, and the Prince of Orange; and of his enterprise afterwards in England*, vol. 2 (London, 1712).

16. The deposed James II's declaration was dated 20 April 1692. The Battle of the Boyne was fought on 1 July 1690.

Chapter Eight

1. *Poems on affairs of State: Augustan satirical verse, 1660–1714*, volume 5, George de Forest Lord (Yale University Press, 1972).
2. Amalia van Solms-Braunfels, wife of Frederik Hendrik and mother of William II of Orange, and Louisa Christina van Solms-Braunfels, who married the Dutch statesman and officer Johan Wolfert van Brederode were sisters, both daughters of Johan Albrecht I of Solms-Braunfels.
3. After Randolph Egerton died, his widow Elizabeth married Randolph's kinsman Charles Egerton, the Earl of Bridgewater's younger brother, thereby putting the family tree in a tangle as Lord William Powlett's mother-in-law became sister-in-law to his own sister Jane, Countess of Bridgewater.
4. Henrietta Powlett was christened on 18 August 1705 at St James's in Piccadilly. Randolph and John were born on 3 October 1707, Egerton John on 10 November 1709 and Scroop on 17 July 1712 (he died the following year and was buried at St James's, Piccadilly). Lord William's daughter Mary, by his first marriage, married Richard Parsons, 1st Earl of Rosse by whom she had two sons and one daughter (Mary died in 1718). The two sons from Lord William's first marriage to Louisa de Caumont were William, born on 1 May 1690 (and died in February 1757) who married a daughter of the 1st Earl of Tankerville and Charles Armand, christened on 1 November 1691 at St Anne's, Soho, who became a major general in the army and married Elizabeth Lewes (of Stanford in Nottinghamshire). Henrietta Powlett married the Honourable Colonel William Townshend, George II's aide-de-camp and Groom of the Bedchamber to Frederick, Prince of Wales. Townshend was a younger son of Charles 'Turnip' Townshend, 2nd Viscount Townshend, who is noted for his innovations and experiments during England's 'Agricultural Revolution', and especially his wholesale and enthusiastic promotion of the humble turnip. He predeceased Henrietta, dying at their home in New Bond Street in 1738. Henrietta died in 1755.
5. *The House of Commons, 1690–1715: Constituencies*, David Hayton (Cambridge University Press, 2002). The 1st Duke of Bolton died on 27 February 1699.
6. Both Frances and John died (of smallpox) before Mordaunt's father, Charles Mordaunt, 3rd Earl of Peterborough. The earldom fell to the eldest of John and Frances' two sons, another Charles Mordaunt, who became the 4th Earl of Peterborough. (www.georgianera.wordpress.com/2017/11/14/the-life-of-viscount-mordaunt-of-avalon) Carey, Countess of Peterborough, née Carey Fraser, was a descendant of Mary Boleyn, as was Lady Frances Powlett on both her mother's and father's side.
7. Another unproven story relating to Henrietta, Duchess of Bolton concerns the notorious London courtesan Teresia Constantia Phillips (1709–65). Con Phillips' adventures were documented in a memoir and she claimed that Henrietta was her godmother. After the death of Con's mother in February 1721, the Duchess of Bolton took her goddaughter into her household and had her educated at a Mrs Filer's boarding school which was located at Prince's Court, Westminster. Soon, however, Con's father made a second marriage to his servant, a 'woman of base qualities'. Con blames her stepmother for causing a rupture between her and the duchess, but possibly Henrietta simply chose not to continue an association with

the family and have any kind of relationship with the low-born Mrs Phillips. In the memoir, *An Apology for the Conduct of Mrs TC Phillips*, an unsubstantiated and vague genealogy is given for Con; she claims descent from the Goodrickes of Yorkshire and makes a claim that her grandfather had married a Powlett heiress who had brought him 250*l*. a year. While the dates don't fit, Sir Henry Goodricke of Ribston (1677–1738) married (in 1707, the year Con claimed her parents married) Mary, only daughter and heir of Tobias Jenkins of Grimston and Mary Powlett, daughter of the 1st Duke of Bolton. If Con Phillips was indeed related by blood to the Duke of Bolton's lineage, then this may explain her claim that Henrietta, third wife of the 2nd Duke of Bolton, was her godmother.

Chapter Nine

1. Horace Walpole to Horace Mann, writing a few days after Lavinia Fenton, Dowager Duchess of Bolton's death on 24 January 1760. *Comedy Queens of the Georgian Era*, John Fyvie.
2. Kilburn, M. (2004, September 23). Powlett [Paulet], Charles, third duke of Bolton (1685–1754), politician. Oxford Dictionary of National Biography. The manor house was built for Elizabeth by her half-brother, Edward VI.
3. General Ross was Charles Ross, son of the 11th Lord Ross, formerly Colonel of the Royal Irish Dragoons.
4. The wedding was held on 22 July 1713. In *Thomas Coram, Gent., 1668–1751* by Gillian Wagner (Boydell & Brewer, 2004), Mary Wortley Montagu is mentioned as Lady Anne Vaughan's distant relative as well as her friend.
5. *Vanilla: Travels in Search of the Ice Cream Orchid* by Tim Ecott (Grove Press, 2007).
6. Lady Mary Wortley Montagu's letters: 24 November 1714 and 8 December 1754.
7. Horace Walpole to Rev. Mr Cole, 21 June 1782.
8. In April 1717, Charles was called up to the House of Lords by the mistaken title of Lord Basing; it was intended that he was called up in his father's Barony of St John but, by accident, the writ was submitted as *Carolo Pawlet de Basing Chr*. This error created a new peerage but at the lowest rank of baron, and so Lord Winchester also became Lord Powlett (or Pawlet) of Basing.
9. Lavinia's parents married – clandestinely at the Fleet – on 6 May 1710; they were described as Peter Beswick, a victualler, and Elizabeth Neal, both from Wapping. Lavinia was christened – as Levinia, daughter of Peter and Eliz Beswick, on 22 October 1710 at St Margaret's in Westminster; the parish register records her birth as 7 October 1710. The old Lincoln's Inn Theatre, formerly the tennis courts, in which Charles II and the 1st Duke of Bolton had seated themselves in the boxes to watch the operas and plays, had been demolished in 1714. The theatre in which Lavinia stepped onto the stage was newly-built, and *The Beggar's Opera* was the inaugural performance.
10. Overseers Accounts 1741–1745 and Poor Rates 1729–1731, Westminster Rate Books, 1634-1900. *Mistress Peachum's Pleasure*, Lisa Hilton. It is now believed Peter the Wild Boy might have suffered from a rare genetic developmental disorder, Pitt-Hopkins syndrome.
11. Charles Powlett's date of birth is recorded on his memorial in the church of St John the Baptist at Itchen Abbas, Hampshire; he was born on 28 December 1728 and

christened at St James's in Piccadilly a week later. Percy may have been christened as James in the same church in August 1730; Horatio Armand was christened on 26 March 1741 at St Alfege in Greenwich.

12. Westcombe House was demolished in 1854. *'Polly Peachum': Being the Story of Lavinia Fenton (Duchess of Bolton) and 'The Beggar's Opera'* by Charles Pearce (quoting Halstead).

13. Hampshire Archives: 11M49/E/T535: Mortgage of a mansion house with adjoining close in Newmarket, Suffolk by Charles, Duke of Bolton, 12 November 1728. The four Canalettos that the 3rd Duke of Bolton is known to have bought are 'View of the Molo, looking north-west with the Palazzo Ducaole' together with a view of the Bacino towards San Giorgio Maggiore, the Canal Grande from Ca' de Mosto and the Canal Grande from Ca' Civran, portraits that were inherited by Lavinia after the duke's death. (Jean Luc Baroni Ltd, Master Paintings and Drawings, archived webpage and Sotheby's catalogue on the sale of a portrait by Canaletto's nephew, Bernardo Bellotto ('Venice, A View of the Molo, Looking West, with the Palazzo Ducale and South Side of the Pizzetta') by Bożena Anna Kowalczyk).

Chapter Ten

1. Catherine Powlett, née Parry, was the great-aunt of Catherine Knatchbull who married Thomas Knight and lived at Chawton House in Hampshire. Thomas and Catherine Knight adopted Edward Austen, the elder brother of the novelist, Jane Austen. Catherine Powlett died aged 49-years and was buried at Edington in Wiltshire on 23 April 1744. In 1754, after his father had become the 4th Duke of Bolton, Harry, the 4th Duke's youngest son, was described in the newspapers as the 'third son', obliquely referring to both his legitimate and illegitimate elder brothers, Charles Powlett and Charles Perry. *Derby Mercury*, 22 November 1754.

2. Before being owned by Winchester, the manor of Edington had belonged for a few years to Sir Thomas Seymour, brother of Henry VIII's third wife Jane Seymour and uncle to Edward VI (Seymour was charged with treason by the young king's regency council and was executed in 1549).

3. Captain Harry Powlett's first command was HMS *Port Mahon*, a newly-launched twenty-gun sixth-rate ship. *The History of Parliament: the House of Commons 1715–1754*, ed. R. Sedgwick, 1970 (via www.historyofparliamentonline.org). Harry Burrard was later created Sir Harry Burrard, 1st Baronet of Walhampton. Curiously, both he and Colonel Charles Powlett (later the 5th Duke of Bolton) received a secret service pension of £500 a year which terminated upon their appointments to a post in the New Forest and as lieutenant of the Tower of London respectively.

4. The Duke of Bolton to the Duke of Newcastle, 25 March 1751, British Library, Add. MS 32724, fol. 212.

5. Although it has been claimed that Lady Anne referred to Lavinia in her will as her 'husband's whore', we find no mention of this in the actual document. Lady Anne Vaughan, Duchess of Bolton, was circumspect and ladylike to the last. NA: PROB 11/795/201, Will of Anne or Ann Dutchess of Bolton, 5 June 1752.

6. The *Scots Magazine*, 1 April 1751, gave the date of the Duchess of Bolton's death as 23 September 1751 but other sources have 20 September, *Caledonian Mercury*; 14 November 1751, *Derby Mercury*; 15 November 1751, *Salisbury and Winchester*

Journal; 4 May, 6 July and 3 August 1752 and CCed, Clergy of the Church of England Database.

7. The barony of Pawlett became extinct with the 3rd Duke of Bolton's death. The 3rd Duke of Bolton died on 26 August 1754.

8. In 1757, Horatio Armand Powlett was apprenticed to Edmund Bochin, a merchant of Sice (now Sise) Lane in the City of London at a premium of £735. NA (IR 1 series) 21, f 42. Lewis de Visme was appointed chaplain to Lavinia, Duchess Dowager of Bolton on 15 October 1754 (CCed Clergy of the Church of England Database). Lewis de Visme (1720–76) later abandoned his career with the church for one in the diplomatic service. Lavinia died on 24 January 1760. Horatio wrote to his brother Percy on the same day from Westcombe. Hampshire Archives, Scrap book of various Powlett and Temple family letters and papers, 72M92/1.

9. Lavinia appeared on stage at Lincoln's Inn Theatre as Polly Peachum in *The Beggar's Opera*. When the Covent Garden Theatre was opened in December 1732, the Lincoln's Inn Theatre was abandoned. Did the 3rd Duke of Bolton manage to acquire his old box from the theatre and have it installed in Wensley Church, no doubt to the grave disapproval of the other parishioners if they knew its origin? The woodwork that makes up the pew is of two dates: the earlier (c.1510) is from the nearby Easby Abbey, acquired after the Dissolution of the Monasteries, and the latter is seventeenth-century. As Lincoln's Inn Theatre was rebuilt between 1710 and 1728, if there is any truth at all in the legend, then the theatre would have had to have reused boxes from the earlier theatre. *A History of the County of York: North Riding*, edited by William Page (London, 1914).

10. Henrietta Powlett and Robert Colebrook married on 12 July 1741; Henrietta died on 22 December 1753 aged 37 and leaving no issue. The cause of death was cancer, from which she had suffered for five years. (Information from the original mausoleum inscription, noted by Reverend Bryan Faussett in 1757; the present inscription neglects to mention the cause of death and gives her age as 36.) Catherine Powlett's wedding to William Ashe took place on 3 February 1749, and her husband died on 11 August 1750. *Select Epitaphs* collected by W. Toldervy, 1755. Lady Catherine Drummond died, without issue, during October 1774.

11. Mary's father, Richard Nunn, a gentleman, had died in 1737; his house, at the east end of Eltham, was subsequently rebuilt and named Park Place Farm. Mary Henrietta Powlett was christened on 23 December 1752.

12. Harry Powlett was christened on 12 July 1754.

13. The Earl of Thanet did provide a London home for Nelly and their sons, but Nelly complained long and hard about having to leave the earl's mansion. If there had been a marriage between Mary Banks and a Mr Brown, it is yet to be discovered. Perhaps there was and this was the bar to Mary becoming a duchess, or maybe there was none and Mrs Brown was an assumed name for the sake of respectability?

14. Kitty Fisher married John Norris, MP in 1766 and died (perhaps of lead poisoning via her use of white make-up) a few months later.

15. Royal Household Establishment Books, 1526–1920.

16. Charles Powlett was born on 15 February and christened at St Marylebone on 11 March 1756.

17. The *Dublin Journal*, 6-10 September, 1757. Suicide seems to have dogged the family: the *General Evening Post*, 19-21 May 1748, reported that 'Yesterday morning, a

servant belonging to Col Perry of Sackville Street, being disordered in his senses, cut his throat; he was carried to the Westminster Infirmary, but 'tis thought he cannot live.' The 57th was renamed as the 55th Regiment of Foot in 1756. Horace Walpole to Sir Horace Mann, 12 November 1779.

18. NA PROB 11/833/14, the will of the Honourable Charles Perry of Sackville Street, 6 September 1757.

19. In time, Mary Henrietta Powlett would become the second wife of John Montagu, 5th Earl of Sandwich.

Chapter Eleven

1. Robert Banks, son of Robert Banks and Jane Wharton, was born c.1711. His mother died in February 1718 and was buried at Bawtry. The marriage of Robert Banks to Ann Horsley took place on 3 January 1722, and the baptisms of their children all took place at Bawtry: John Horsley (who changed his surname to Horsley in later life, becoming John Banks Horsley) on 30 September 1722; Mary on 4 September 1724; Barnabas on 13 June 1726; Francis on 17 November 1727; and Joseph on 27 July 1729.

2. Robert Banks of Bawtry to Joseph Banks (1695–1741) in St James's Square.

3. NYCRO, Powlett Papers ZBO IX 1/22/101.

4. The marriage between Captain Francis Banks and Christian Green took place on 21 February 1760 and was witnessed by the bride and groom's brothers, William Green and John Banks Horsley. *London Chronicle*, 2 October 1760. Christian died on 29 September 1760. It would be the first but not the last family will from which Captain Francis Banks benefitted. Thirteen years later, he was again named as executor and sole beneficiary to his second cousin, Captain George Banks of the Coldstream Guards; Captain George Banks was one of the two sons of Joseph Banks' (1695–1741) second marriage to Catherine Collingwood. He was Sir Joseph Banks' step-uncle.

5. The house on Grosvenor Square that belonged to the 5th and 6th Dukes of Bolton is now numbered 37.

6. James Brydges, Marquess of Carnarvon, was later the 3rd Duke of Chandos. Most sources seem to agree that the duel was fought at Marylebone.

7. *London Evening Post*, 22-24 April 1760. In 1761, Sir Simeon Stuart was returned for Hampshire together with Henry Bilson Legge. Thomas Gray to Dr Wharton, 22 April 1760 (www.thomasgray.org).

8. *Derby Mercury*, 25 September 1761.

9. *St James's Chronicle*, 15-17 November 1763.

10. *The History of Parliament: the House of Commons 1754–1790*, eds L. Namier, J. Brooke, 1964.

11. The information about the marriage made by the 5th Duke of Bolton and Mary Banks Brown comes from Thomas Christopher Banks, often noted as a charlatan but a man who claimed to be Mary's relation. (Sir Joseph Banks corresponded with T.C. Banks for some time in a similar vein.) In his work *Baronia Anglica concentrate; or, a Concentrated Account of all the Baronies commonly called Baronies in Fee*, vol. 2 (Ripon, 1843), Banks, when discussing the validity – or otherwise – of the Fleet registers as evidence in a court case, wrote a footnote saying that 'Charles,

Duke of Bolton was married to Mrs Mary Brown, at May Fair Chapel, – the entry was abstracted, – the cause is well known. The duke's demise, by his own hands, followed not long after.' Unfortunately for us, Banks failed to elaborate further on 'the cause'.

12. *The Grenville Papers*, volume 2. In July 1766, a year after the Duke of Bolton's death, William Pitt became prime minister; had Bolton still lived, he might yet have received his Garter.

13. The other executor was George Durnford, Esq. of Winchester. The 5th Duke of Bolton was godfather to Durnford's son, Charles.

14. *The Critical Review, or, Annals of Literature*, volume 20, 1765.

Chapter Twelve

1. HMS *Oxford* was launched in June 1674 as a fifty-four-gun ship; she was rebuilt in the 1720s as a fifty-gun vessel and relaunched in 1727.

2. *Derby Mercury*, 24 October 1755.

3. *Ipswich Journal*, 21 and 28 February 1756.

4. *Dr. Johnson's Mrs. Thrale, Autobiography, letters and literary remains of Mrs. Piozzi*, edited by A. Hayward (T.N. Foulis, Edinburgh & London, 1910).

5. For Amelia's birth: the *Scots Magazine*, July 1768.

6. George III Calendar papers for 1765, GEO/MAIN/160, Royal Archives. Bolton's new wife connected him by marriage to the king's favourite, the Earl of Bute, as Bute's daughter Mary was the wife of Katherine Lowther's brother James. Although, as James Lowther ignored his wife in favour of a string of mistresses, it is debatable how useful this familial link proved to be.

7. Bolton's face in the portrait is underpainted. The painting passed down to his granddaughter Viscountess Templeton and is now in the collection of the Metropolitan Museum of Art in New York. The miniaturist Richard Cosway used the Cotes portrait as the basis for a miniature portrait of the duke painted in 1793.

8. Lord Holland, writing to George Selwyn from Lyon on 2 May 1770, said, 'You saw Mr Delmé the night before he shot himself: I suppose you took care to see him the night after; I suppose he had his reasons, but if his wife does not guess, or does not tell, you will never know them.' *George Selwyn and His Contemporaries, 2: With Memoirs and Notes*, 1843. Peter Delmé (who committed suicide on 10 April 1770) lived at No. 36 (now No. 41) Grosvenor Square; the 5th Duke of Bolton at No. 32 (now No. 37). The manors conveyed to Delmé were Edington Rector, Edington Romsey, Tinhead Rector and Tinhead Romsey.

9. *The Diaries of a Duchess, extracts from the diaries of the 1st Duchess of Northumberland* (Hodder & Stoughton, 1926). *Derby Mercury*, 16 June 1769, the *Scots Magazine*, vol. 31, 1769 and *Music and Theatre in Handel's World: the family papers of James Harris, 1732–1780* by Donald Burrows and Rosemary Dunhill (OUP 2002); the masked ball and supper at Hackwood took place on 1 June. *Salisbury and Winchester Journal*, 12 June 1769. A domino was a silk cloak, usually black and often with a hood, which covered the whole body.

10. NA, C 211/20/P111, Lady Amelia Powlett, spinster of Petworth, Sussex: commission and inquisition of lunacy, into her state of mind and her property, 2 June 1809. Amelia Powlett was buried on 5 June 1816.

Keightley, Thomas, *The History of England*, vol. 3 (Whittaker & Co., 1839)

Kiste, John van der, *William and Mary: Heroes of the Glorious Revolution* (The History Press, 2017)

Kitson, Frank, *Old Ironsides: The Military Biography of Oliver Cromwell* (Weidenfeld & Nicolson, 2004)

Loades, David, *The Life and Career of William Paulet (c.1475–1572), Lord Treasurer and First Marquis of Winchester* (Ashgate Publishing, 2008)

Mackintosh, Sir James, *History of the Revolution in England in 1688: Comprising a View of the Reign of James II, from His Accession, to the Enterprise of the Prince of Orange* (Carey, Lea & Blanchard, 1835)

Madden, Frederic, Bandinel, Bulkeley and Nichols, John Gough (eds.), *Collectanea Topographica et Genealogica*, vol. 4 (London, 1837)

Major, Joanne and Murden, Sarah, *An Infamous Mistress: The Life, Loves and Family of the Celebrated Grace Dalrymple Elliott* (Pen and Sword History, 2016)

Miall, James Goodeve, *Yorkshire Illustrations of English History* (Hall, Smart & Allen, 1865)

Milton, John, *The Poetical Works of John Milton: with notes of various authors* (edited by the Reverend Henry J. Todd), vol. VII (London, 1809)

Muilman, Teresia Constantia, *An Apology for the Conduct of Mrs T.C. Phillips*, volume 1 (London, 1761)

Newman, Peter Robert, *The Old Service: Royalist Regimental Colonels and the Civil War, 1642–46* (Manchester University Press, 1993)

Newman, Peter Robert, *The Royalist Army in Northern England 1642–45* (PhD thesis, University of York, 1978)

Pearce, Charles, *'Polly Peachum': Being the Story of Lavinia Fenton (Duchess of Bolton) and 'The Beggar's Opera'* (Brentano's, New York, 1913)

Peck, William R., *A topographical history and description of Bawtry and Thorne, with the villages adjacent* (Thomas and Hunslet, 1813)

Plowden, Alison, *Women All On Fire: The Women of the English Civil War* (Sutton Publishing, 1998)

Read, Sara, *Maids, Wives, Widows: Exploring Early Modern Women's Lives 1540–1740* (Pen and Sword History, 2015)

Reilly, Emilia Georgiana Susanna, *Historical Anecdotes of the Families of the Boleynes, Careys, Mordaunts, Hamiltons, and Jocelyns, arranged as an elucidation of the Genealogical Chart at Tollymore Park, etc.* (1839)

Reresby, Sir John, *The Memoirs of the Honourable Sir John Reresby, Baronet and Last Governor of York: containing several private and remarkable transactions, from the Restoration to the Revolution inclusively* (1734)

Reresby, Sir John, *The Memoirs of Sir John Reresby of Thrybergh, Bart., MP for York &c, 1634–1689* (London, 1875)

Riley, W. Edward and Gomme, Laurence (eds), *Survey of London: Volume 5, St Giles-in-the-Fields*, Pt. II (London, 1914)

Roberts, George, *The life, progresses and rebellion of James Duke of Monmouth & to his capture and execution*, volume 1 (London, 1844)

Russell, Lady Rachael, *Some account of the life of Rachael Wriothesley, Lady Russell* (London, 1819)

Sheppard, F.H.W. (ed.), 'Grosvenor Square: Individual Houses built before 1926', in *Survey of London: Volume 40, the Grosvenor Estate in Mayfair, Part 2 (The Buildings)* (London, 1980, British History Online)

Smith, John Thomas, *The Streets of London with anecdotes of their more celebrated residents* (Richard Bentley, 1849)

Smith, William James (ed.), *The Grenville Papers: being the correspondence of Richard Grenville Earl Temple, K.G., and the Right Hon. George Grenville, their friends and contemporaries*, vols 2 and 3 (John Murray, 1853)

Smollett, Tobias, *The Adventures of Roderick Random* (London, 1748)

Somerset, Anne, *Queen Anne: The Politics of Passion* (Harper Press, 2012)

Spencer, Charles, *Killers of the King: The Men Who Dared to Execute Charles I* (Bloomsbury, 2014)

Spencer, Charles, *Prince Rupert: The Last Cavalier* (Weidenfeld & Nicolson, 2007)

Thoroton, Robert and Throsby, John, *Thoroton's History of Nottinghamshire*, vol. 1 (London, 1797)

Tinniswood, Adrian, *Behind the Throne: a domestic history of the royal household* (Jonathan Cape, 2018)

Tomlinson, John R.G. (ed.), *Additional Grenville Papers 1763–1765* (Manchester University Press, 1962)

Toms, Jan, *To Serve Two Masters: Colonel Robert Hammond, the King's Gaoler* (Partizan Press, 2015)

Uglow, Jenny, *A Gambling Man: Charles II and the Restoration* (Faber & Faber, 2010)

Underdown, David, *Aristocratic Faction and Reformist Politics in Eighteenth-Century Hampshire: The Election of December 1779* (Huntington Library Quarterly, vol. 68, no. 4, 2005)

Victoria County History, *A History of the County of Buckingham*, vol. 4 (London, 1927)

Walford, Edward, *'Mayfair', in Old and New London: Volume 4* (London, 1878, British History Online)

Walpole, Horace, *Letters of Horace Walpole, Earl of Orford to Sir Horace Mann, his Britannic Majesty's Resident at the court of Florence, from 1760 to 1785*, vol. 1 (Lea & Blanchard, 1844)

Walpole, Horace, *The Letters of Horace Walpole, vol. VI, 1778–1797* (Richard Bentley, 1840)

A History of the County of Wiltshire: Volume 8, Warminster, Westbury and Whorwellsdown Hundreds (Originally published by Victoria County History, London, 1965)

Periodicals and contemporary publications:

A Description of the Siege of Basing Castle kept by the Lord Marquisse of Winchester for the Service of His Maiisty [sic] Against the Forces of the Rebells Under Command of Colonell Norton (Oxford, 1644)

The Speeches and Prayers of some of the late King's Judges (1660)

London's dreadful visitation: or, a collection of all the Bills of Mortality for this present year: beginning the 27th of December 1664 and ending the 19th of December following: as also the general or whole year's bill. According to the report made to the King's most excellent Majesty. (1665)

The Cook's and Confectioner's Dictionary: or, the accomplish'd Housewife's Companion, revised and recommended by John Nott, Cook to his Grace the Duke of Bolton (London, 1723)

The new peerage, or, Ancient and present state of the nobility of England, Scotland, and Ireland: containing a genealogical account of all the peers, whether by tenure, summons, or creation, their descents and collateral branches, their births, marriages, issue, chief seats, paternal coats of arms, crests and supporters, together with literal translations of the mottoes : to which is added, the extinct peerage, comprehending an authentic account of our peers from the earliest times, and an alphabetical index of all noble family names, and titles of their elders sons: in three volumes, volume I (London, 1784)

Archival sources:

National Archives: C 11/1778/31, Pawlett v Parry

Lieutenant General Cromwell's Letter to the Honourable William Lenthall Esq., Speaker of the House of Commons; of the Storming and Taking Basing-House (London, 1645)

Hampshire Archives: Powlett/Dukes of Bolton papers

North Yorkshire County Records Office: Powlett/Dukes of Bolton papers

Calendar of State Papers, Domestic Series, of the reign of Charles II, 1667–1668, preserved in the State Paper Department of Her Majesty's Public Record Office. Vol. 8: Nov 1667-Sept 1668

Oxford Dictionary of National Biography:

(2004, September 23). Scrope, Emanuel, earl of Sunderland (1584–1630), nobleman

Andrews, J. (2009, May 21). Napier, Richard (1559–1634), astrological physician and Church of England clergyman

Baldwin, O. & Wilson, T. (2008, January 03). Fenton [née Besswick; married name Powlett or Paulet], Lavinia, duchess of Bolton (1710–1760), actress and singer

Hosford, D. (2004, September 23). Paulet [Powlett], Charles, first duke of Bolton (1630/31–1699), politician

Hughes, J. (2009, January 08). Stafford [née Boleyn; other married name Carey], Mary (c.1499–1543), royal mistress

Hutton, R. (2004, September 23). Paulet, John, fifth marquess of Winchester (1598?–1675), royalist nobleman

Kelly, J. (2008, January 03). Powlett, Thomas Orde-, first Baron Bolton (1746–1807), politician

Kilburn, M. (2008, January 03). Paulet [Powlett], Charles, second duke of Bolton (c.1661–1722), politician

Kilburn, M. (2004, September 23). Powlett [Paulet], Charles, third duke of Bolton (1685–1754), politician

McCreery, Cindy (2008, September 04). Fischer [married name Norris], Catherine Maria [known as Kitty Fisher] (1741?-1767)

Peacey, J. (2004, September 23). Wallop, Robert (1601–1667), politician

Turbutt, G. (2008, January 03). Frescheville [Frecheville] family (per. 1518–1682), gentry

Online sources:

Pepys diary (www.pepysdiary.com)

City of Westminster Coroners: Coroners' Inquests into Suspicious Deaths, 1765 (www.londonlives.org)

Huskinson, Thomas W., *The Summer Excursion: 1908* (Transactions of the Thoroton Society, 12 (1908) (via www.nottshistory.org.uk)

Horace Walpole's Correspondence, Yale Edition, The Lewis Walpole Library (images. library.yale.edu/hwcorrespondence)

Walker and Nussey – Royal Apothecaries, 1784–1860 by John T.M. Nussey (www. cambridge.org)

Thomas Anson and Shugborough by Andrew Baker (www.heardmusic.co.uk)

Manuscript sources:

History, vol. 56, no. 187 (June 1971: G.E. Aylmer, 'Was Oliver Cromwell a member of the army in 1646–7 or not?'

An Aspect of European Diplomacy in the Mid-Eighteenth Century: The Diplomatic Career of the Fourth Earl of Rochford at Turin, Madrid, and Paris, 1749–1768; thesis presented for the Degree of Doctor of Philosophy in History in the University of Canterbury, Christchurch, New Zealand by G.W. Rice MA, March 1973

Letters of Lady Rachel Russell; from the manuscript in the library at Woburn Abbey, 9th edition (London, 1826)

Index